FAMOUS AIRCRAFT OF THE
NATIONAL AIR AND SPACE MUSEUM

VOLUME 1
EXCALIBUR III
The Story of a P-51 Mustang

VOLUME 2
THE AERONCA C-2
The Story of the Flying Bathtub

VOLUME 3
THE P-80 SHOOTING STAR
Evolution of a Jet Fighter

VOLUME 4
ALBATROS D. Va
German Fighter of World War I

VOLUME 5
BLERIOT XI
The Story of a Classic Aircraft

VOLUME 6
BELLANCA C.F.
The Emergence of the Cabin Monoplane
in the United States

VOLUME 7
de HAVILLAND DH-4
From Flaming Coffin to Living Legend

VOLUME 8
MOONLIGHT INTERCEPTOR
Japan's "Irving" Night Fighter

VOLUME 9
FOCKE-WULF Fw 190
Workhorse of the Luftwaffe

Focke-Wulf Fw 190

Workhorse of the Luftwaffe

Jay P. Spenser

PUBLISHED FOR THE
National Air and Space Museum
BY THE
Smithsonian Institution Press
WASHINGTON, D.C., AND LONDON
1987

LIBRARY OF CONGRESS CATALOGING IN PUBLICATION DATA

Spenser, Jay P.
  Focke-Wulf Fw 190, workhorse of the Luftwaffe
  (Famous aircraft of the National Air and Space Museum; v.9)
  Bibliography: p.
  1. Focke-Wulf Fw 190 (Fighter planes) I. Title. II. Series
UG1242.F5S6377 1987   358.4'3   86-6000267
ISBN 0-87474-877-1

Cover: Painting of the Fw 190 by Craig Kodera
©1987 National Air and Space Museum

To Mike Lyons
Modeler, master craftsman, and wonderful friend,
who will always be remembered by his colleagues
at the National Air and Space Museum

Contents

Foreword

The history of air warfare is punctuated with the sudden appearance of new aircraft. Such events can make a dramatic impact on the course of a war. The goals are always the same—to achieve a decisive technological edge and to meet the combat requirements of the battlefield.

Jay Spenser's third contribution to the Famous Aircraft Series, *Focke-Wulf Fw 190: Workhorse of the Luftwaffe,* is an authoritative account of one air weapon that made a dramatic debut in World War II and profoundly influenced the course of the air war.

The author attains a balanced historical perspective on the Fw 190, covering its combat life both as a fighter and as the lethal close support machine that retarded or repulsed armored Soviet thrusts against the German army. Beyond providing an overview of the Fw 190 and its development, he breaks ground by presenting new material on close support versions of the Focke-Wulf. To cover this lesser-known history, Spenser tells how *Luftwaffe Schlachtgruppen* (ground attack units), newly equipped with Fw 190s after 1943, faced the enormous demands of the Russian campaign. His account is based on an exhaustive research of existing sources, including numerous German-language primary sources and in-depth interviews with German pilots who flew the aircraft. Through this larger history of German ground attack aviation, a tradition that began in World War I, the roles of the Fw 190 F and G are viewed for the first time in their proper historical perspective. The Focke-Wulf Fw 190 emerged in World War II as one of the more versatile military aircraft—a fighter, ground attack machine, long-range fighter bomber, and reconnaissance aircraft. In assuming these multiple duties, it underwent numerous modifications; Jay Spenser reconstructs for the reader the brilliant design work of Kurt Tank and others who made the airplane a dramatic success. Beyond this technical overview, he sheds light on another aspect of the story—the combat life of pilots who flew Focke-Wulfs in Russia. The result is a balanced and highly readable account of this German aircraft from its inception to the end of the war.

The story of the Fw 190 is not told in isolation. Spenser's historical account is linked directly to the 1983 restoration of the National Air and Space Museum's Fw 190 F-8. His research, as it turns out, had concrete benefits: the author located and obtained a rare bomb rack missing from the NASM machine. *Focke-Wulf Fw 190: Workhorse of the Luftwaffe* reflects the unique character of the Famous Aircraft Series, which blends original historical research with Museum restoration, both here fascinatingly recounted.

VON D. HARDESTY, PH.D.
Curator
National Air and Space Museum
Washington, D.C.

Preface

The Focke-Wulf Fw 190 is a legendary airplane that proved a deadly foe to Soviet, British, and American aircraft alike. Eventually dominated by Allied numerical superiority and attrition in German resources (especially in pilots), it was nevertheless a formidable fighting machine that ranks among the best produced during the war. Newer, faster, and more maneuverable than the Messerschmitt Bf 109 (the Luftwaffe's other first-line fighter), the sleek Focke-Wulf was above all versatile.

The National Air and Space Museum's Fw 190F exemplifies one use of Fw 190s. When the infamous Junkers Ju 87 Stuka grew too old for service, it was the Focke-Wulf fighter that shouldered the burden of ground attack on the eastern front. The Museum's recently restored machine served with Schlachtgeschwader 2, flying air-to-ground close support missions in the U.S.S.R. and Hungary. Also known as the "Immelmann" wing, SG 2 was the oldest ground attack wing in the Luftwaffe; NASM's Fw 190 F-8 fought with this unit under the command of legendary Stuka pilot Hans Ulrich Rudel.

Much has been written on the specifications, performance, and many versions of the Focke-Wulf Fw 190, with particular emphasis on its employment as a fighter. The opposite is true of its less glamorous use as a ground attack machine. This volume attempts to address the lack. Instead of giving another "nuts and bolts" description of the airplane, it seeks to place German ground attack operations in a clear historical perspective. Key personalities, tactics, and the day-to-day life of the front-line *Schlachtflieger* (ground attack pilot) are all elements of the story. German terms appear throughout to familiarize the reader with proper terminology. The nouns are capitalized according to the convention of that language, and unit and aircraft designations follow proper German nomenclature except in direct quotes. In the frequently questioned case of the designation "Bf 109" versus "Me 109"—both of which are to be found in original Luftwaffe documents—the former has been chosen because Bayerische Flugzeugwerke was the name of the Messerschmitt company at the time the legendary Bf 109 first flew. To assist the reader, a glossary of German terms appears as appendix 1. Translations from German-language primary source material are the author's own.

Acknowledgments

For much of the primary source material so essential to this project, the author is singularly indebted to Dr. James H. Kitchens, III, of the USAF Historical Research Center, Maxwell Air Force Base, Alabama. Equally heartfelt is his gratitude to valued colleague Dr. Von D. Hardesty, to whose excellent book *Red Phoenix* the reader is directed for a balanced and insightful understanding of the Soviet air force in World War II.

Among those to be thanked for contributing expertise, photographs, and other assistance are Arno Abendroth; Gebhard Aders; Horst Amberg; John and Carole Bessette; Rich Boylen, National Archives and Records Administration, Suitland, Maryland; Dr. Horst Boog, Militärgeschichtliches Forschungsamt, Freiburg; General Mark E. Bradley; Bundesarchiv, Koblenz; Volkert Bünz; Ken Chilstrom; Joachim Dressel; Jeff Ethell; Uwe Feist; John Gaertner; Gen.Lt. a.D. Adolf Galland; Werner Girbig; Jack Ilfrey; John Jarmy; Dr. A. G. Johnson; Lt. Col. George Lamb, USAF (Ret.); Dr. Heinz Lange; Richard J. Lee; Brigadier General Gustav E. Lundquist, USAF (Ret.); Barry Mahon; Colonel George Manolis, USAF; Hans Justus Meier; Heinz J. Nowarra; William R. O'Brien; George Petersen; Peter Petrick; Konrad Pingel; Major General Osmund Ritland, USAF (Ret.); Eugene P. Roberts; Peter Rodeike; Dipl.-Ing. Hans Sander; Hans Seebrandt; Fritz Seyffardt; J. Richard Smith; Deborah Spenser; Halvor Sperbund; Karl Stein; Barrett Tillman; Ray Toliver; Peter Traubel; John J. Voll; Maj. Gen. Harold E. Watson; and Dipl.-Ing. Eberhard-Dietrich Weber.

Among his colleagues at the National Air and Space Museum, the author is particularly indebted to Mark Avino, Ron Davies, Debbie Douglas, Phil Edwards; Dale Hrabak; Rick Leyes; Donald S. Lopez; Robert C. Mikesh; F. Robert van der Linden; Larry Wilson; and E. T. Wooldridge, Jr. Finally, he must thank Michelle Smith of the Smithsonian Institution Press for her excellent job editing this manuscript.

Prototype of a famous series, the Focke-Wulf Fw 190 V1 first flew on June 1, 1939. Fitted with an eighteen-cylinder 1,550 hp BMW 139 radial engine, it had a ducted spinner cooling fan which was replaced by the NACA cowling illustrated here. (SI A 48623-B)

1

Origin and Development of the Fw 190

The first Fw 190s entered combat in the late summer of 1941, shocking the already beleaguered British with greater speed and heavier armament than their Supermarine Spitfire Mark V. That such performance could be packed into such a trim German fighter was astounding. It was a beautiful machine, lean and elegantly lethal. As its unofficial name *Würger* (butcher bird) suggested, it inspired both dread and admiration.

The origins of the Fw 190 date back to late 1937, when the *Reichsluftfahrtministerium* (German Air Ministry) issued a contract to Focke-Wulf Flugzeugbau for the development of a new single-seat fighter. Overseeing the project was the head of Focke-Wulf, Professor Kurt W. Tank. A major figure in the German aircraft industry, Tank was also a brilliant design engineer and noted test pilot. His company put forward two proposals for the new machine, one version to be powered by the liquid-cooled Daimler-Benz DB 601 and the other by the twin-row radial BMW 139 power plant. With 600-series Daimler-Benz engine production taken up by Messerschmitt Bf 109s and Bf 110s, and the Junkers Jumo 211—Germany's other liquid-cooled engine series—needed for Heinkel He 111 bombers and Junkers Ju 87 Stukas, the German Air Ministry surprisingly approved the latter proposal despite traditional antipathy toward radial power plants.

The Fw 190 V5k taxies to the runway in 1940. This fifth prototype was fitted with the fourteen-cylinder 1,600 BMW 801, an engine which—although larger and heavier—had far greater development potential than the BMW 139. The k in the designation, standing for klein, *denotes the small wing being tested. (SI A 43422-A)*

Work began in earnest on what was initially to be merely a fall-back interceptor to the vaunted Messerschmitt Bf 109 fighter, already famous from the Spanish Civil War.

Dipl.-Ing.[1] Hans Sander, a gifted Aachen-trained aeronautical engineer, was to play a central role in the development of the new fighter. Hired by Tank in 1937, Sander had been given a free hand to set up a flight test facility at the company's airfield at Langenhagen, just north of Hannover. Under his guidance, the facility became a miniature factory with its own design department for quick fixes, machine shops for the manufacture or modification of parts, and active flight test division with civil and Luftwaffe test pilots. The accelerated wartime development of Focke-Wulf fighters is in large measure attributable to Hans Sander's department.

Sander was also one of Germany's foremost test pilots, whose many flight hours had earned him the special civilian title of Flugkapitän. After taking the Focke-Wulf Fw 190 up for the first time on June 1, 1939, Sander landed favorably impressed with the handling and performance of the prototype, but he recognized that the tightly cowled engine installation was unsatisfactory. The design was reworked to incorporate the heavier BMW

Fw 190 A-3 W.-Nr. 471 is shown in flight early in 1942, with Kurt Tank at the controls. (SI 86-3839)

A compact machine of war, this Fw 190A prototype taxis to the runway at the Focke-Wulf Flight Test Facility, Langenhagen, Germany, late in 1941. (SI 86-588)

Looking ready for action, preproduction Fw 190s are run up for a Focke-Wulf Flugzeugbau publicity photograph in 1941. (SI 77-12503)

801, a newer type with far greater development potential. This unit produced approximately 1,600 hp at 2,400 rpm at 14,000 feet and featured a two-stage supercharger. It was fuel-injected but otherwise generally similar to the American Pratt & Whitneys that Bayerische Motorenwerke had license-built before the war.

The design philosophy behind the Fw 190 was to attach a big radial engine, encased in a NACA cowl[2] only 4.3 feet in diameter, to the smallest and simplest airframe possible. Measures taken to provide adequate cooling for the engine included extensive baffling, a twelve-bladed geared fan at the front, and lateral ducts low on the cowling sides to channel air back to the rear cylinders.

The propeller was a constant speed VDM unit, geared to run at slightly over half the engine RPM. Its diameter of 10.9 feet, small for so much power, was offset by relatively wide blades. These large-area blades in great measure accounted for the Fw 190's superb climb characteristics; American P-47s and B-17s were among the Allied aircraft that later enjoyed a similar increase in climb performance when fitted with "paddle-bladed" propellers.

The fuselage was of semi-monocoque construction, with four longerons and twenty-one stringers covered with flush-riveted Alclad skin. The cockpit was well laid out with full gyro instruments, and the pilot sat on his parachute in an unusual but comfortable attitude with his legs extended. Under his seat were two self-sealing fuel cells of rubberized fiber shell construction. The bulletproof windshield was sharply swept back to present minimal frontal area—and resultant drag—to the slipstream, and the close-fitting sliding canopy was a single formed piece of laminated plexiglass that provided excellent visibility to the rear. Airflow made it impossible to crank the canopy back in flight, so the unit was made jettisonable by means of an explosive cartridge that broke the track guide on the top deck to destroy the canopy's anchorage.

For strength and lightness, the wing was a single-piece unit with a heavy I-beam main spar that was routed rearwards at the center section to

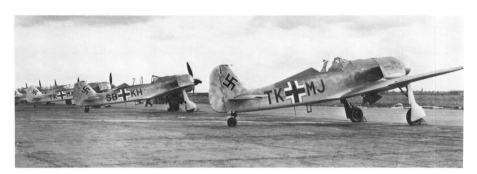

Fw 190A deliveries to the Luftwaffe began early in 1941. Immediately popular with its pilots, the new fighter proved superior to the Spitfire Mark V when the two types clashed for the first time on September 27, 1941. (SI 86-590)

provide space for the retracted wheels. The rear spar was similar in construction, but much lighter. The flaps were of the older split type, and the ailerons were balanced Frise units. As all fuel was stored in the fuselage, there was room in the wings for four guns and ammunition.

The empennage featured relatively small horizontal and vertical surfaces. Rudder and elevators, like the ailerons, had ground-adjustable tabs only. The horizontal stabilizer was electrically adjustable from a −3 degree to a +5 degree angle of incidence. Because controls were very light (with the exception of the elevators, which would load up at very high speeds), conventional trim tabs were not required.

In addition to 20-mm aircraft cannon in the wings, early production Focke-Wulf fighters had two 7.92-mm Rheinmetall MG 17 machine guns atop the fuselage, just forward of the cockpit. Comparable to American .30-caliber weapons, these light guns were replaced with more powerful 13-mm MG 131 (roughly .50-caliber) machine guns in A-7 and later Focke-Wulfs. Courtesy of Joachim Dressel. (SI 86-3815)

An Fw 190 F-8/R1 at Langenhagen shows the exceptionally clean lines and minimal frontal area of the Focke-Wulf design. The wide-track landing gear facilitated ground handling, making the Focke-Wulf less prone to ground looping than the Messerschmitt Bf 109. Courtesy of George Petersen via Jeff Ethell. (SI 82-11842)

Prominent in the design was a graceful landing gear, whose long-travel oleo struts swung out to provide a wide and stable ground track. The tailwheel retraction mechanism, which relied entirely on springs and a cable connection to the right main gear for actuation, was especially ingenious.

This was the first fighter to be virtually all electric. The fundamental idea was that small electric lines are harder to shoot out than hydraulic lines. Electric power was supplied by a 24-volt generator supplemented by a battery behind the pilot's armored seat. These drove the landing gear, flaps, and stabilizer trim, and energized the inertial starter (a hand crank, stowed in the rear fuselage compartment, was also provided for emergency starting).

German aircraft were traditionally heavily armed with excellent weapons, and the diminutive Focke-Wulf was no exception. Basic armament, standardized early in production, was two 20-mm Mauser MG 151 cannon

13

Wearing the codes KO+MD, this prototype for the Fw 190 A-3/R1 Trop (tropical) series displays extra inlets and filters for rear cylinder bank cooling. Like many Fw 190 fighter subvariants, it is fitted with wing and fuselage bomb racks. Courtesy of George Petersen via Jeff Ethell. (SI 82-11844)

near the wing roots synchronized to fire through the propeller arc, and two shorter 20-mm Oerlikon MG FF cannon farther out, just beyond each landing gear attachment point. Fuselage armament consisted of a pair of synchronized 7.92-mm MG 17 machine guns just forward of the windshield. In later models of the Focke-Wulf, more effective 13-mm MG 131s replaced these rifle-caliber guns.

After successful trials at Erprobungsstelle Rechlin (the Luftwaffe's equivalent of Wright Field or Farnborough), the Fw 190 entered service with Jagdgeschwader 26 in France. The first clash between Fw 190s and Spitfires came at the end of August in 1941, and showed the Focke-Wulf to be superior in almost every regard to the British fighter.

Fw 190A production increased quickly. Focke-Wulf's factories at Tutow, Cottbus, Sorau, Schwerin, and Neubrandenburg were augmented by license production by Ago at Oschersleben, Arado at Brandenburg and Warnemünde, and Fieseler with two plants near Kassel. By the time Fw 190s escorted the German battle cruisers *Scharnhorst* and *Gneisenau* and the heavy cruiser *Prinz Eugen* through the English Channel in the spring of 1942, Fw 190 production exceeded 250 machines a month.

Accelerated by wartime pressures, the A-series underwent steady improvement. The A-4 of early 1943 offered superior combat speeds as its BMW 801 D-2 engine could briefly produce 2,100 hp with methanol-water injection. The A-5 had its engine moved 15 cm (6 inches) farther forward to solve the chronic problem of engine overheating; versions of this model were the first Fw 190s to be fitted with a central bomb rack for fighter-bomber operations. A-5s played a key role in the staggeringly heavy bomber losses suffered by American Eighth Air Force bombers in the two Schweinfurt missions of August and October 1943.

Successive improvements during 1943 led to the A-6 through A-8, which offered heavier armament and improvements in radio equipment. In each case, subseries versions displayed a variety of armament configurations, including rockets and 30-mm cannon. The Fw 190 A-7/R6, for example, carried 21-cm W.Gr. 21 rockets for use against American bomber formations.

Design of the Fw 190 called for the extremely tight cowling of a BMW 801 radial power plant. With the help of a forced cooling fan (visible behind the spinner), Focke-Wulf designers achieved unparalleled success, producing the most aerodynamically trim radial-engined fighter of World War II. This A-5, W.-Nr. 410 739, lacks armament and features cheek intakes to boost performance at altitude. Courtesy of George Petersen via Jeff Ethell. (SI 82-11843)

This Fw 190 A-5, modified to Fw 190 F-8/R1 configuration for armament trials at Langenhagen, is equipped with ETC 71 wing bomb racks. Later refinements to this series included the substititution of ETC 50 wing racks, the elimination of cheek intakes, and the addition of a bubble canopy. Courtesy of George Petersen via Jeff Ethell. (SI 82-11860)

Neither the B- nor C- series progressed beyond the prototype stage; the next Focke-Wulf fighter to enter service was the Fw 190D. Called "Dora" by its pilots, this markedly different model was powered by a 1,776-hp Junkers Jumo 213A inverted-vee power plant. Although the cowling housing this liquid-cooled engine was very long, it retained a radial engine appearance because it had an annular radiator. Weight and balance considerations dictated that the rear fuselage also be lengthened.

The Fw 190 D-9 series, better at altitude and substantially faster than short-nosed Focke-Wulfs, quickly found favor after its introduction in the fall of 1944. This excellent machine is widely considered the finest piston-engined interceptor to have entered Luftwaffe service in meaningful—although relatively small—numbers.

There was also a ground attack version of the Dora, the D-12, which was fitted with a 2,060-hp Jumo 213F engine.

Prototype for the A-9 series, Fw 190 V35 BH+CF awaits its pilot for a test flight at Langenhagen. Courtesy of George Petersen via Jeff Ethell. (SI 82-11856)

A Focke-Wulf Fw 190 A-5/U8, loaded with two 300-l drop tanks and a 250-kg bomb, prepares for a long-range bombing mission from a snowy airfield. Courtesy of George Petersen via Jeff Ethell. (SI 82-11858)

The E-series, a projected reconnaissance variant, was never built. The final two production models were the F and G ground support aircraft, which entered service before the D model. The Fw 190G, called Jabo-Rei,[3] was an extended-range fighter-bomber. It entered service before the F, and was in effect a redesignated continuation of the bomb rack–equipped A model variants. These ground attack versions were produced concurrently with the later A-series.

The final production series for ground attack was the Fw 190F Schlachtflugzeug. This model may generally be recognized by its bulged cockpit hood, which gave it a more pleasing appearance than the flat-canopied models as well as needed headroom, a feature it shared with the Fw 190D. The F differed from the G primarily in favoring armor over range.

Fw 190 V53, W.-Nr. 170 003, was a prototype for the Fw 190D series. Powered by a twelve-cylinder inverted-vee 1,776 hp Junkers Jumo 213A power plant, this long-nose Focke-Wulf was easily distinguished from shorter radial-engined versions despite the "radial" appearance of its annular radiator. This machine is heavily armed with four 20-mm MG 151 cannon in the wings and two 13-mm MG 131 cannon in the fuselage. Courtesy of George Petersen via Jeff Ethell. (SI 82-11851)

The early-style national insignia and flat canopy reveal this Fw 190, W.-Nr. 582 075, to be an early production example of the F-8 ground attack series. It is shown here at Königsberg/Neumark in the summer of 1944. Courtesy of Peter Petrick. (SI 85-18826)

To offset this increased armor weight, the outboard 20-mm cannon were deleted. After the Fw 190 F-3, the first version built in any numbers, the relatively weak 7.92-mm MG 17 fuselage machine guns were replaced with 13-mm (roughly .50-caliber) MG 131s; this and other improvements led to the Fw 190 F-8 and F-9.

By far the most important of the F versions was the F-8, which in standard F-8/R1 configuration had four ETC 50 wing racks and an ETC 501 fuselage rack. The F model would provide most late-war tactical air support, going low and hitting hard in the face of fierce ground fire. Near war's end a few F-9 aircraft were built with more-powerful BMW 801TS engines. F-10 and subsequent projected developments never materialized.

At the end of the war, one other highly advanced version of the Fw 190 was built. The ultimate development of the design, this was the Ta 152 (the new "Ta" prefix was for Kurt Tank, in recognition of his remarkable achievements). The Ta 152H, a high-altitude version, ranks as perhaps the fastest piston-engined fighter of the war. It entered combat on a very limited basis in the spring of 1945.

Tow bar attached to the tailwheel, Fw 190 V20 sits ready to fulfill its role as a Ta 152C prototype. Cowl flaps, cannon bulges on wing near the root, split flaps, and the Junkers Jumo 213 supercharger intake show well in this view. Courtesy of George Petersen via Jeff Ethell. (SI 82-11847)

2

Schlachtfliegerei

chlacht means slaughter. *Schlachtfliegerei* means ground attack, the most dangerous and least glamorous part of wartime flying. There is no room here for romantic illusion, no pretense of chivalry; one is down on the deck where the targets—people, vehicles, installations, and fortifications—may be clearly seen. The ground attack pilot is exposed to every bit of flak, every machine gun, every rifle, every pistol. Denied him is the acclaim accorded fighter pilots—the chances of winning fame as a Schlachtflieger are as slim as those of survival.

Ironically, very little is generally known of either the beginnings or the subsequent development of German ground attack operations. To understand the National Air and Space Museum's Focke-Wulf Fw 190 F-8 and its place in history, one must examine the origins, tactics, machines, and men that together created Germany's aerial close support arm.

During World War II, the Luftwaffe excelled in air-to-ground close support operations because this role best matched the German concept of how aerial warfare should be waged. In this view, the military airplane was primarily a tactical weapon subordinate to the requirements of the battle-fields below. Strategic use of military aviation was not appreciated by Nazi Germany in time to influence its conduct of the air war.

These terms bear defining: Strategic operations are those in which aircraft act independently of armies to bring the war home to the enemy; such operations generally take the form of long-range bombardment. This philosophy, practiced during World War II by the United States and Great Britain,[1] seeks to deny the enemy the means to wage war, not just meet him on the field of battle. Tactical air operations, on the other hand, are those performed in conjunction with broader offensive or defensive measures on or near the front lines. These are short-ranged, usually directly in support of ground forces.

Because Germany pursued a doctrine of tactical military aviation in World War II, its aircraft almost invariably had short ranges. Different philosophies produce different machines; for the Luftwaffe, manufacturers were only required to give their airplanes sufficient flight endurance for operations from airfields near the immediate combat arena. These builders of airplanes were happy to dispense with additional range requirements for the simple reason that every gallon of fuel not carried meant six pounds less weight, a savings that translated directly into speed, maneuverability, armament, and bomb load.

HISTORICAL ANTECEDENTS

It was in World War I that Schlachtfliegerei began. Halberstadt and Hannover two-seaters were among the airplanes that Germany used against ground targets during that war, but it was not until 1918 that there entered service an airplane specifically designed for the task. This first true ground attack machine was the Junkers J 1, an all-metal aircraft known as the Mule.

The first airplane built specifically for ground attack, the Junkers J 1 (company designation J 4) flew operationally in 1918.

There were no less than thirty-nine *Schlachtstaffeln* (fighter squadrons) on the front at the time of the Armistice.[2] While military interest in ground attack carried into the postwar years, public attention was diverted by a different use of the airplane that engendered a reaction similar to (and long since superseded by) the present fear of nuclear weapons. This perceived threat to world peace was the large bomber; the influential voice of Giulio Douhet[3] lent a hard edge to its emotional perception in the 1920s and 1930s as a weapon against which no defense was possible.

During World War I, Germany pioneered such advances as all-metal structures and fully cantilevered wings.[4] This superiority continued into the postwar years, as best evidenced by the Junkers F 13 monoplane of 1919. The first airliner of modern low-wing configuration, the F 13 featured all-metal construction and an enclosed passenger cabin. In an era of open-cockpit wood and fabric biplanes—scarcely sixteen years after the Wright brothers made their historic 1903 flight—the F 13 represented an advance so revolutionary as to be almost incomprehensible; it would be ten more years before the Northrop Alpha, a plane combining similar features with subsequent refinements, would appear in the United States.

At such German companies as Junkers and Rohrbach, a new generation of engineers was already rising to continue this tradition of technological excellence. If the 1930s saw leadership in aviation shift to the United States, the decade also witnessed the rise to prominence of such legendary figures in the German aviation industry as Willi Messerschmitt, Ernst Heinkel, and Kurt Tank.

Although the Treaty of Versailles compelled Germany to disarm, a covert move toward rearmament began in the early years of the Weimar Republic, long before Adolf Hitler brought his National Socialists to power in January 1933. Hitler accelerated the rearmament, pulling Germany out of both the League of Nations and the World Disarmament Conference, and by 1934 it was clear to the world that Germany had embarked upon an unprecedented military build-up.

In 1922, Germany and the U.S.S.R.—then the two pariah nations of Europe—had signed the Treaty of Rapallo. This agreement laid the groundwork for covert cooperation in which both countries profited: Germany obtained raw materials from Russia, as well as military training facilities beyond the eyes of the Allied Control Commissions that enforced the Carthaginian peace of Versailles. The Soviet Union, in return, obtained expert flight training and the latest German aircraft.

Under Rapallo's camouflage, the Junkers company built a huge aircraft factory at Fili, near Moscow, where modern construction techniques were introduced to Soviet apprentices. Actual military flight training took place primarily at the more remote location of Lipetsk, where joint German-Soviet maneuvers were routinely conducted. Military aviation received particular emphasis at Lipetsk; it was here that the Germans experimented secretly with all types of aircraft and air tactics. The roles and strategies defined would guide both powers in the coming war and substantially influence the evolving German ground attack arm.

With the Luftwaffe and the Soviet air force drawing largely from a common pool of experience, it is hardly surprising that their wartime air forces were so similar. In a larger sense, there was another important factor: both countries were continental military powers shaped by a history of inter-European warfare. This fundamental similarity worked to consolidate their perception of the airplane as a weapon to complement ground operations. Airplanes enhanced conventional warfare; they did not transcend it. As a result, both the German and Soviet air forces remained almost exclusively tactical throughout World War II.

During Nazi rearmament in the 1930s, Hitler and his generals were deeply impressed by U.S. Navy experiments in dive bombing, a form of aerial bombardment more accurate than conventional level bomb dropping. Here was a tool that precisely fit their military needs. With the integration of dive bombing into Blitzkrieg, the basic elements for conquest were at hand.

The Spanish Civil War brought about the rebirth of Schlachtfliegerei. This bloody conflict, which served as the proving ground for modern weapons and tactics, saw in 1937 the first German air operations in support of troops since World War I. Freiherr Wolfram von Richthofen, a World War I ace in the Jasta[5] of his famous cousin Manfred, the Red Baron, commanded the famous Legion Kondor in Spain. A strong believer in close aerial support, this lesser-known von Richthofen was the guiding force behind these early air-to-ground operations. The tactics and procedures he developed—well suited to the primitive conditions of Spain—would become those of the Blitzkrieg two years later.

Germany's first new airplane expressly designed for ground attack was the Junkers Ju 87 Stuka.[6] A rugged instrument of war first flown in 1935, the Ju 87 is today too readily dismissed for its lack of speed and unsuitability to later wartime conditions, twin failings stemming from two implicit planning misconceptions. These were that the war would be a short one and that Germany would always retain air superiority. A contradictory reality would only too late force the selection of the superb Focke-Wulf Fw 190 as the Ju 87's successor.

During the war in Spain, von Richthofen employed Arado Ar 68s, Heinkel He 51s, and Henschel Hs 123s for coordinated air-to-ground support operations, but not the new Junkers Ju 87s he received in 1938. He ordered these dive bombers to roam freely over the battlefields to attack targets of opportunity and soften up the enemy. Although effective, such operations represented only indirect and uncoordinated ground support.

The need for a separate ground attack arm had not yet been perceived by the High Command, so Schlachtfliegerei found itself lumped with the

A German pilot in a Mae West and summer flight gear climbs into an Fw 190 with the Wagnerian name Siegfried. Painted below the name is an Infanterie-Sturmabzeichen (combat infantry assault badge), which reflects this airplane's ground support mission. Courtesy of Uwe Feist. (SI 85-18266)

Behind this informally attired German soldier sits a bomb-carrying Fw 190 A-7/R6. Courtesy of Schmitt via Peter Petrick. (SI 85-18827)

fighter (*Jagd*) branch of the Luftwaffe. The new Stukas, however, were obviously a bomber type to be assigned to the German air force's bombardment (*Kampf*) arm. Von Richthofen's arbitrary exemption of the new Ju 87—the best ground attack machine then in service—from coordinated ground support duties in Spain further compounded official misapprehensions as to the Ju 87's proper role, drawing a distinction where none existed. For most of World War II, consequently, the Stuka would shoulder ground attack duties but be officially excluded from the ranks of Schlachtfliegerei.

In the *Wehrmacht* (armed forces) at the start of World War II, ground attack units were subordinate to and directly controlled by the *Heer* (German army). That ground force commanders enjoyed instant air support accounted in great measure for the successes of *Blitzkrieg* (lightning war). The combination of armor, fluid movement, and tactical air support in Czechoslovakia, Poland, Yugoslavia, France, and the Low Countries shocked a world unprepared for the horrors brought by modern military aviation.

Public perceptions of the effectiveness of the Ju 87 were emotionally heightened by newsreel images of irresistible Stuka swarms crushing all opposition to Nazi conquest. The reputation of this aircraft reached its zenith during the Battle of France in 1940, again under the direction of Wolfram von Richthofen, who was now in command of the VIII. Fliegerkorps. Also called "Fliegerkorps Richthofen," this special tactical air command within the Luftwaffe spearheaded the Blitzkrieg in the west.

During the Battle of Britain, the illusion of invincibility finally gave way to reality. Stukas were brought down in droves when they attacked convoys in the Channel and Thames Estuary, or bombed radar stations situated along the coast of East Anglia. Like the Messerschmitt Bf 110, which was also vulnerable to modern single-seat, single-engine fighters, the vaunted Ju 87 was shown to be unquestionably obsolete. Especially crippling in this aerial assault was the short range of Luftwaffe bombers and fighters; the otherwise superb Messerschmitt Bf 109 was particularly limited in this regard, spending far too little time over England to be effective.

Although Germany enjoyed tremendous numerical superiority in aircraft, it lacked a comprehensive strategy for their employment. The Royal Air Force, in contrast, had just instituted a fully integrated radar ground control system that maximized the effectiveness of every precious Spitfire and Hurricane. Germany's defeat in the Battle of Britain, today viewed as the turning point of the European war, brought the realization that the Luftwaffe was equipped with the wrong airplanes for a long war in which targets were not always near.

There would be many such painful realizations during the war, all stemming from a chronic failure of Nazi leadership to come to realistic terms with the war of its making. Despite its monolithic façade, the Wehrmacht never achieved true integration of its disparate elements, many of which were badly structured. Far from forming an efficient war machine, Germany's individual services suffered from a lack of coherent definition, which produced inefficiencies of duplication, jurisdictional disputes, and blatant working at cross purposes. The Luftwaffe's ground attack arm was no exception.

OPERATION BARBAROSSA

June 22, 1941, is a date of unparalleled significance in the history of tactical air warfare. On this day, some 2,000 Luftwaffe planes swept into the Soviet

21

Union and caught three-quarters of that country's air force—some 7,500 aircraft—on the ground. Just behind this devastating onslaught marched an army of 3,800,000 men. Operation Barbarossa, the biggest Blitzkrieg yet, was on and Germany and Russia were at war.[7]

They were the bitterest of enemies, fascist Germany and communist Soviet Union, each viewing the other as antithetical and inimical despite the outward similarities of their totalitarian systems. There was no Geneva Convention between the two powers; it would be a bitter and cruel war, fought on a huge scale rarely appreciated in the West.

German ground forces made rapid breakthroughs, secured territory, and encircled Soviet troops along a vast front running from the Baltic Sea all the way into Romania. The three main thrusts of conquest were toward Leningrad in the north, Moscow in the center, and Kiev and the Ukraine in the south.

A formation of Junkers Ju 87B dive bombers flies over the Soviet Union sometime in 1942. (SI A-5224)

Despite its initial great gains, the German Wehrmacht failed to seize a decisive victory in 1941. Most of the aircraft destroyed by the Luftwaffe were obsolete machines such as the I-15 and I-16 fighters and DB-3 bomber, and the U.S.S.R. suffered minimal attrition in flight crews as these machines were primarily destroyed on the ground. The greatest element of hope for the Soviet air force was that a transition to newer aircraft was already in progress.

The Soviet aircraft industry, just beginning to produce these first-line machines, undertook in July 1941 a massive relocation. This arduous move, unprecedented in scale, put most Soviet strategic aviation targets east of the Urals, far beyond the range of Germany's tactical bombers and fighters. Stalin now had a secure base from which to develop the Soviet Union's industrial potential. He had an air force still numbering some 2,500 aircraft and—in contrast to Germany—great reserves of manpower.

Perhaps the greatest Soviet advantage was the vastness of Russia, the scale of which is difficult to appreciate. By the end of 1941, the front ran two thousand miles from Murmansk to the Black Sea; at its peak in 1942, it would reach three thousand miles in length. The other physical obstacle was the severity of Russian winters; although these worked great hardships on both sides, they denied Germany momentum while granting the Soviet Union desperately needed time.

The realization at the end of the first summer campaign that it would not after all be a short war brought about a major shift in Wehrmacht structuring and tactics. Whereas ground attack units had formerly been subordinate to—and directly controlled by—the army, they now reverted to Luftwaffe control. This change reflected a crisis of the severest magnitude: a knockout blow not having been dealt, Germany now faced a protracted war for which it was unprepared, along a spreading front whose size precluded full aerial support.

Junkers Ju 87 production increased in 1940 for lack of a viable successor. This dive bomber—however devastating it was in the Balkans, Crete, or North Africa—was nearing the end of its service life everywhere outside the U.S.S.R. There the very scale of the land, which otherwise worked against the Wehrmacht, gave it operational freedom.

It was initially planned that the Messerschmitt Me 210 would replace the Ju 87. The Battle of Britain had clearly demonstrated the vulnerability of twin-engine, multi-seat fighters like the Bf 110, so Messerschmitt's newer plane built to this formula would be the next-generation ground attack plane rather than a *Zerstörer* (destroyer).[8] Hopes for the Me 210, already dim in 1942, soon disappeared altogether when this dangerous machine was deemed a total failure.[9]

Simultaneously, the battles for Moscow and Stalingrad, two major campaigns in 1942, made it clear that Luftwaffe ground attack operations were inadequate. While von Richthofen's VIII. Fliegerkorps did well, the same could not be said for similar units assigned to other Luftflotten in Russia. "They had far fewer successes than the Korps Richthofen," Generals Adolf Galland and Hubertus Hitschold observed in a joint assessment. "When Richthofen wasn't there, things went wrong."[10]

A bomb-laden Junkers Ju 87D takes off from a snowy airfield in the U.S.S.R. in 1944. Stukas were the backbone of German ground attack on the eastern front through most of World War II. (SI 86-777)

It was felt in some quarters that von Richthofen's reputation and his personal pride in his elite corps had served to mask critical inadequacies in ground attack tactics. At the start of the Stalingrad Offensive in July 1942, he was promoted to the command of Luftflotte 4. By the fall of that year, heavy losses and an erosion of air and ground superiority meant that there was much blame to be apportioned, but von Richthofen had already abandoned the foundering ship of his design. A Generalmarschall by war's end, he died of a brain tumor shortly after V-E Day.

Another strong personality emerged in 1942 to champion the retention of established methods of ground attack. This was the young Stuka pilot Hans Ulrich Rudel. Flying up to twenty missions a day from forward airfields, Rudel became the master of ground attack in all its many forms, particularly the destruction of tanks. A twenty-eight-year-old colonel with more than 2,500 missions to his credit by war's end, Rudel had destroyed some five hundred to seven hundred tanks in addition to more conventional targets such as bridges, ships, supply columns, airfields, command posts, and communication centers. His accomplishments and political leanings found particular favor with Adolf Hitler, who awarded him the Golden Oak Leaves with Swords and Diamonds to his Knight's Cross, a distinction accorded no other Luftwaffe pilot.

Soviet T-34 and Stalin tanks were always a particular problem on the long and occasionally sparsely manned Russian front. The Luftwaffe's first tank-buster was the twin-engined Henschel Hs 129. Unwieldy and never available in meaningful numbers, the slow Hs 129 (reportedly just 22 mph faster than the Ju 87) suffered particularly from the shortcomings of its Gnome-Rhone engines.[11] This power plant frequently failed in the dusty conditions of southern Russia—a problem particularly acute at Stalingrad—and was easily set ablaze in attacks. Moreover, the Henschel's 30-mm or 37-mm cannon lacked sufficient punch to deal Soviet tanks a lethal blow.[12] As the Hs 129's small airframe was structurally too weak to accept other more-powerful engines, service use of the type was limited to just one Gruppe.

War forced both sides to adapt and improvise. One modification to emerge from Stalingrad was the Ju 87G, a special version of the trusty Stuka with underwing 37-mm cannon pods. These stopgap tank killers were supplied to Stukagruppen 1, 2, 3, and 77 as a tenth squadron. Called Panzerbekämpfungsstaffeln, these special squadrons each had twelve cannon-equipped Stukas along with four bomb-carrying versions for flak suppression. In St.G. 2, Hans Ulrich Rudel flew the Ju 87G with devastating effect. He pioneered the rear attack, where their engines and thinner armor made Russian tanks more vulnerable. It must be emphasized, however, that the Ju 87G was painfully obsolete and even clumsier than Stukas not fitted with underwing cannon pods. It was never available in great quantity, a fact that aggravated the German failure to produce the successor required for a prolonged war.

The spring and summer of 1943 saw two additional German thrusts, both ably countered by a revitalized U.S.S.R. From April until the beginning of June there were raging dogfights on a massive scale over the Kuban River area of the North Caucasus. A restructured Soviet air force, now equipped with updated fighters like the Yakovlev Yak-7 and Yak-9, confronted some of the Luftwaffe's best units, among them JG 52 with top German aces Erich Hartmann (352 victories) and Gerd Barkhorn (301 victories).

Air supremacy hung in the balance at Kuban, but the outcome of these unprecedented air battles was decided even before they began. Whatever

Engine roaring, an Fw 190 A-5 of Schlachtgeschwader 1 climbs away from an East European runway. Courtesy of Karl Stein. (SI 85-14226)

A view of the same aircraft in flight shows the 1,105-lb SC 500 bomb hanging from the faired ETC 501 bomb rack. Bombs were generally delivered in shallow dives rather than in the very steep dive of the Stukas. Courtesy of Karl Stein. (SI 85-14227)

Fw 190 F-8/R1 Schwarze 9 (black 9), lined up with other aircraft of SG 2 in Hungary, is readied for a mission along the collapsing Russian front. This photograph was taken early in 1945. Courtesy of Hans Obert via Peter Petrick. (SI 85-18818)

the relative strengths and skills of the combatants, the Luftwaffe was doomed to failure because Germany could no longer afford to pursue a war of attrition. In contrast, the "Red Falcons"[13] had great reserves of manpower and equipment. Moreover, earlier Soviet failings in training had been addressed; Soviet pilots now fought aggressively with tactics copied from the Luftwaffe itself.

Kursk, a city located on a strategic north-south railway line below Moscow, lent its name to the second phase of the eastern war in 1943. On July 5, German forces began a pincer operation to isolate and eliminate the large Soviet salient around the Ukranian city of Kursk, in the central portion of the front. If successful, the operation would consolidate German lines and result in the capture of many Soviet forces.

The tide turned very quickly against the Wehrmacht when the Soviets launched a successful counteroffensive in July and August. The Soviet air force, which undertook its first large-scale air offensives of the war, was instrumental in this success. At Kursk, Ilyushin IL-2 Shturmovik ground attack aircraft were extensively employed for the first time, although some examples had already entered service at the time of the German invasion.

Ivan N. Kozhedub, who made his combat debut over Kursk, would finish the war the top Soviet—indeed the top Allied—ace with sixty-two victories. Just behind him with fifty-nine victories was Alexander I. Pokryshkin, a brilliant aerial tactician who performed the crucial task of drastically reworking Soviet fighter operations to the realities of World War II. Pokryshkin scored most of his victories in the Bell P-39 Airacobra, an American fighter provided by the thousand through Lend-Lease; because of the 37-mm aircraft cannon fitted to some P-39s, the type also found great favor in the ground attack role where it proved effective.

For Germany's Schlachtflieger, late 1943 was a trying time. Despite shortages of men and materiel, they were being asked to do ever more in an increasingly hostile environment. There was no denying that drastic measures must be taken, and taken quickly, if Germany was to retain any capability for aerial support of its beleaguered ground troops.

Another F-8 of SG 2 taxis out for a mission in the winter of 1944–45. The wheel covers and fuselage bomb rack have been removed from this machine, which carries 50-kg bombs on its wing racks. Courtesy of Hans Obert via Peter Petrick. (SI 85-18816)

Two SG 2 Fw 190 F-8/R1s taxi out for a mission against Soviet forces. The central bomb rack of Schwarze 2 *(black 2) supports an AB 250 cluster bomb. In addition to temporary snow camouflage, this machine sports a yellow "V" under the left wing and a yellow fuselage band. Courtesy of Hans Obert via Peter Petrick. (SI 85-18820)*

Especially dangerous to their operations were Soviet flak and small arms fire, which had reached withering proportions. While German troops would hit the dirt and leave defense to their flak units when attacked by Ilyushin IL-2 Shturmoviks, Soviet troops observed no such specialization. "With the Russians," proclaimed Stuka pilot Oberstleutnant Ernst Kupfer, "everyone and everything shoots!"[14]

In fact, in the fall of 1943 two distinct measures were taken that ushered Germany into the second phase of its eastern war. The first was a long-needed and far-reaching restructuring of its ground attack forces. They now became a separate branch of the Luftwaffe instead of part of its fighter and (Stukas only) bomber commands. For the workhorse Ju 87, which had performed most of the ground attack for four years, it meant at last formal acceptance into the ranks of Schlachtfliegerei.

The second measure was the selection of the Focke-Wulf Fw 190 fighter as the Stuka's replacement. The reasons for this choice were many: First, bomb rack modifications had already been perfected for fighter-bomber versions of the A-series. Second, the Focke-Wulf had a wide, strong landing gear. Third, its air-cooled engine rendered it substantially less vulnerable than planes fitted with liquid-cooled engines whose cooling systems could be punctured by ground fire (hundreds of Stukas had been lost in this way). Fourth, the Fw 190 was the best fighter in the Luftwaffe's inventory; even with extra armor and bomb racks it offered respectable performance. Fifth, and most critical, it was already in large-scale production.

The Focke-Wulf was a compromise in one sense. It lay between an ideal machine for which there was no development time and the hard realities of existing aircraft production capacity. Primarily because of the limited supply of BMW 801 radial engines, substantially fewer Fw 190s were being built than Messerschmitt Bf 109s. Although some Messerschmitt fighters found their way into ground attack units, they were considered unsuitable because of their narrow undercarriages, liquid-cooled engines, and relatively poor visibility.

General Erhard Milch, Generalluftzeugmeister der Luftwaffe, lent his support to the selection of the Fw 190, but cautioned that *Reichsverteidigung* (defense of the Reich) must come before all other considerations.[15] Home defense did, in fact, have priority over the needs of external war

Photographed in Hungary in February 1945, this Fw 190 F-8 of III./SG 10 prepares to deliver needed supplies in a parachute-equipped drop container on the main bomb rack. On the left wing racks are a standard SC 50 bomb and, nearer the camera, a cannister of unknown function. Like SG 2, some SG 10 Focke-Wulfs are known to have worn a yellow "V" under the wing. Courtesy of Ernst Obermeier via Peter Petrick. (SI 85-18825)

theaters. Throughout 1943 and 1944, the growing burden of Allied day and night bombing forced fighter production to increase at the expense of other aircraft types, turning the Luftwaffe ever more into a defensive instrument. For these reasons, initial efforts to reequip front-line ground attack units with Fw 190Gs (the G model preceded the F model into combat) at the start of 1943 were abortive. Now in the fall of 1943, with a desperate need for the newer aircraft on the eastern front, Milch could only promise that the transition would take place "within three-quarters of a year."[16]

This conversion to the Fw 190 never fully took place, despite a great increase in fighter production late in World War II. In late June 1944, General der Flieger Karl Koller wrongly speculated the reason might be that "ground attack units are based on fields that are not suitable for the Fw 190."[17]

A more valid reason, interestingly enough, was that the top ground attack pilots resisted relinquishing their trusted mounts. Just as Germany's top fighter aces often chose to keep their Bf 109s rather than fly the newer Fw 190s, so the older Schlachtflieger hesitated to tamper with the formula of their past successes. By mid-1944, nine out of ten Staffeln in Hans Ulrich Rudel's wing flew Fw 190s, yet Rudel himself continued to fly Stukas right up to the end.

Rudel and other experienced pilots knew that the Ju 87 was a phenomenally accurate ground attack machine. Its low speed, stability, and dive brakes made it possible for the best pilots to regularly hit pinpoint targets. Stuka veteran Karl Stein remembers briefings at Warsaw at the start of 1945 when he and fellow pilots were told the specific windows in buildings through which to hurl their bombs.[18]

An SG 2 Focke-Wulf runs up its engine. Natural metal cowls with colorful nose bowls were typical of front-line aircraft late in the war, when primitive forward airfields offered only very basic facilities. To simplify engine changes, everything supported by the engine mount was replaced as a single unit. Called a Kraft-Ei (power egg), the removed unit—including engine, cowling, oil cooler, hydraulic reservoir, and accessories—was then repaired at leisure and reused. Courtesy of Hans Obert via Peter Petrick. (SI 85-18815)

The life of a ground attack pilot was one of hardships and frequent moves from one unimproved airfield to another. Here, pilots of II./SG 2 (the second group of the Immelmann wing) congregate at their alert hut in Hungary, early in 1945. Courtesy of Gebhard Aders via Peter Petrick. (SI 86-3819)

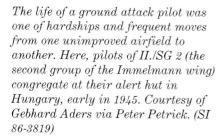

Oberstleutnant Ernst Kupfer (shown here as a Major), a brilliant leader and formative thinker in air-to-ground tactics, became the first General der Schlachtflieger in the fall of 1943. A doctor of law and former cavalry officer, Kupfer was a legendary Stuka pilot. Courtesy of Heinz J. Nowarra. (SI 86-3820)

"Only Rudel and a few other experts mastered the technique of diving attacks against tanks," asserts a joint statement made by Generals Galland and Hitschhold. "Precisely because they did, however, the development of anti-tank cannon, etc., was delayed. . . . This mistake had especially unpleasant consequences in the east, because it came at precisely the time when it would have been necessary to find an answer to the increasing number of Russian armored vehicles. Research and production for ground attack was therefore given a very low priority."[19]

Organizational restructuring of ground attack as a separate branch of the Luftwaffe called for the creation of a General der Schlachtflieger. Major Ernst Kupfer, doctor of law and legendary Stuka pilot, became the first general of ground attack operations[20] on September 1, 1943, at which time he was also promoted to Oberstleutnant. A Heidelberg graduate, Kupfer learned to fly at age thirty-two and flew his first combat missions in the Balkans and over Crete. Despite being older than his peers, he was a popular pilot, respected for his intelligence and leadership abilities.

Kupfer flew in Operation Barbarossa from the very first day, earning a Knight's Cross in November 1941 and becoming commander of St.G. 2's second group the following spring. Shot down behind enemy lines three times in quick succession, he returned to base in each instance, although the last crash left him with severe head injuries. After a partial convalescence, he returned to the front in February 1943 to take over St.G. 2, which he led during the Kuban and Kursk fighting. During the former, several other Stuka and fighter groups were assigned to his command, and after the successful Soviet counteroffensive at Kursk he consolidated all remaining groups into one effective combat unit known simply as *Gefechtsverband Kupfer* (Battle Group Kupfer). Under his leadership, this unit halted a major Soviet tank breakthrough, allowing German troops critically needed time to withdraw.

That he had survived was remarkable (he flew his six-hundredth mission on July 2, 1943, his thirty-sixth birthday). His combat days were behind him as he settled into his new headquarters just outside Berlin, in a large building on Rangsdorf Lake that had been built as a restaurant for the 1936 Olympic games.[21]

Nine days after his arrival, Kupfer made an important speech on ground attack operations and the need for the Fw 190. Although the gravity

Flowers and champagne await an SG 2 pilot upon completion of his two-hundredth operational sortie on the eastern front. Courtesy of Gebhard Aders via Peter Petrick. (SI 86-3821)

of the situation in the east was still not fully appreciated, the growing specter of an eventual Soviet drive to Berlin left the High Command well disposed to listen. Kupfer's presentation, made to Erhard Milch and other high-ranking officials, was therefore particularly influential and served to delineate the basic course of ground attack operations for the remainder of the war.[22]

"The Ju 87 is no longer acceptable in any theater of war, not even in the east," Ernst Kupfer began. "To give an example, my Stukageschwader lost eighty-nine crews in eight months. That represents a yearly average of 100 percent. This result would—if we were to so continue for another year—mean the extermination of all Stukas."[22]

Flak, the greatest enemy of the Schlachtflieger, would now be more actively combated since it accounted for 80 percent of Stuka losses whereas enemy fighters claimed only 20 percent. Despite the intensity of the Soviet flak, Kupfer stressed the need for fast and maneuverable planes rather than ones rendered unwieldy by heavy armor. He dismissed the Soviet IL-2

Not all duty stations were devoid of comfort for Schlachtflieger on the Soviet front. Here pilots enjoy chauffered service. The mouse emblem on the Horch Kfz 69s armored personnel carrier is that of II./SG 1. Courtesy of Gebhard Aders via Peter Petrick. (SI 86-3818)

armored attack plane as obsolete, now able to operate only with substantial fighter escort.

"We created the Tiger, the Panther, the Ferdinand with enormous strength, thick plates of armor," Kupfer stated, using tanks as an analogy. "But we saw from the air time and again in the slaughters at Kursk, Belgorod, and Orel that even these tanks could be stopped by Flak [anti-aircraft guns] and by Pak [anti-armor guns]."

Speed and maneuverability were the only answer; they would obviate the need for fighter escort, freeing the latter for combat to regain air superiority. The new ground attack plane should also be small in order to present flak gunners with a difficult target; it should be single-seat, now all the more urgent because of critical crew shortages; and it should have an armament consisting of 20-mm cannon. These would be adequate against live targets and lightly armored vehicles; tanks, another matter entirely, would be the concern of special aircraft with heavier armament.

The heaviest bombs that Schlachtflieger would require would be 250-kg (551-lb) types. Targets invulnerable to such attacks would be turned over to the Luftwaffe's twin-engine bombers. Kupfer cited an attack against a Soviet stronghold in Stalingrad as an example of Schlachtflieger being called up to do what was really a job for the heavies. His Stukas dropped 500-kg bombs on it for forty-five minutes, but even bull's-eyes were not enough to drive the Soviets from their underground lair.

For troop columns, truck convoys, and other "live" targets, he stressed that large clusters of the smallest bombs available were the most effective. These should weigh one to four kilograms each, eight at the most. "A type of bomb that would be especially important for us," he observed, "would be one with shrapnel effect, one that goes off two or three meters above the ground and throws little steel and iron splinters around in a circle."

The degree to which war had become businesslike in its inhumanity was also illustrated in Kupfer's call for an effective fire bomb. He described attempts using every means imaginable to set grain ablaze in the Orel Hills, all of which were in vain. "We must be in a position to set woods and grain fields on fire," he stated adamantly, "to strip aside enemy camouflage at which the Russians are masters. . . . I myself tried to set very dry reeds on fire in the Kuban region. There was a flash of fire that went high, then it was out."

Regarding tactics, he said that Stukas now made vertical dives only once in every five hundred attacks. This method, once so effective, leaves the airplane far more vulnerable after pulling out than a shallow diving attack in which momentum remains to carry one to safety. He acknowledged that the vertical dive was still more accurate, but stated that better reflex gunsights would offset the difference. His aircraft, Kupfer complained, were fitted with the same gunsights they had used in 1938.

Radios were a similar problem. The fact that Luftwaffe ground attack aircraft were not better equipped for their mission was an expression of the continual failure at higher levels to develop comprehensive policies of broad interservice cooperation. "We must have a radio with which we can talk with the ground, also with the tanks," Kupfer said. "Even now such a thing is completely unavailable. I can talk with neither reconnaissance planes, nor fighters, nor tanks with the radio that's in the Ju 87."

Kupfer stated that a key function of Schlachtfliegerei must be to halt tank breakthroughs across the long and tenuous front. One new tactic he encouraged was to seek out and destroy the light armored vehicles that accompanied Soviet tanks to carry extra fuel. They were far more vulner-

Painted similarly to the NASM Fw 190 F-8, this aircraft of SG 2 receives help taxiing for takeoff from a snow-encrusted airfield in Hungary, early in 1945. Removal of wheel fairings was a common practice in snow and mud conditions. Courtesy of Hans Obert via Peter Petrick. (SI 85-18817)

Another view of the same machine shows the yellow "V" under the left wing. This bright marking may have been a quick identification aid designed to minimize fire from "friendly" troops on the fast-collapsing Russian front of late World War II. Courtesy of Hans Obert via Peter Petrick. (SI 85-18819)

Oberst (later Generalmajor) Hubertus Hitschhold served as the second and last General der Schlachtflieger after the death of Ernst Kupfer. Like his predecessor, Hitschhold was a veteran Stuka pilot and former SG 2 member. Courtesy of Ray Toliver. (SI 85-18828)

able than the tanks themselves to aerial attack, and their destruction would greatly compromise the effectiveness of marauding Soviet armor.

The strongest demand of the new general of ground attack centered on the Focke-Wulf Fw 190. "We must as soon as possible, I would say at once, begin converting Ju 87 units to the Fw 190. The personnel situation in Stuka flying is such that we are 'playing the last record.' Just since July 5, I have lost two wing commanders, six squadron commanders, and two group adjutants, all of whom had flown over six hundred missions. This level of experience cannot be replaced. Units from the squadron level up cannot be filled, so bad is it. . . . We cannot afford to waste the few who are left."

Another indication of the attrition suffered in ground attack units was his description of entire wings with just thirty-five operational aircraft rather than the normal two hundred. "I have squadrons," he affirmed, "with a strength of one aircraft."

At the conclusion of his address, Ernst Kupfer pressed for the elimination of the terms *Stuka* and *Schlacht*, believing all ground attack operations should come under the more sensible heading of *Nahkampffliegerei* (close support operations). This proposal was vetoed by Milch who protested that "*Nahkampf* doesn't sound good,"[29] adding that *Schlacht* held considerable special meaning for the Luftwaffe. The issue was further settled when it was announced that Reichsmarschall Hermann Göring "does not want the word *Stuka* to disappear." As was so often the case with fascism, appearances mattered more than any realistic considerations.

Oberstleutnant Ernst Kupfer was not to see his plans carried out. On an inspection tour of the Balkans in December 1943, he died when his Heinkel He 111 crashed into a mountain north of Dojran Lake in Greece. Posthumously promoted to Oberst, he was awarded Swords to his Knight's Cross with Oak Leaves.

The next General der Schlachtflieger held the post until the end of the war. Hubertus Hitschhold, a newly promoted Oberst (later Generalmajor), was a veteran of Poland, France, England, the Balkans, Crete, Italy, and Russia. Just thirty-one years old when he took up his new duties at Rangsdorf at the start of 1944, he was an equally ardent exponent of Focke-Wulfs in air-to-ground operations (his own unit had converted to the Fw 190G as early as February 1943).

Hitschhold took over at a time of crisis. On the logistical side there remained shortages of fuel, 20-mm ammunition, and tires for the Fw 190. In terms of airplanes, however, the picture was brighter: Germany's miraculous late-war boom in fighter production meant that by 1944 there were enough Fw 190s to reequip Schlachtgruppen at the rate of two every six weeks. Training was primarily performed at Königgrätz. Just a few pilots would attend, then return to their units to check out their Kameraden as the sleek new machines arrived; this system allowed the receiving units to remain operational instead of standing down.

For the Schlachtflieger, the Focke-Wulf Fw 190 offered renewed hope. The F and G models (and a few bomb rack–equipped As) were augmented toward the end by long-nosed Ds. All were rugged and effective in combat, although deficient on three counts: First, Fw 190s could not operate from fields as crude as those suitable for Stukas; ironically, retreat ameliorated this problem by bringing into play many of the excellent Luftwaffe airfields prepared in earlier years.

Second, the Fockes had no special bomb sights. Pilots judged bomb drops with Revi gunsights, antiquated reflector units that were still standard in Luftwaffe fighters despite the fact that new gyroscopic sights (similar to those used by the British and Americans) already existed in Germany. Examples of these special gyro sights, provided experimentally to a few top pilots, had long before demonstrated their worth, but few ever reached the front.

Third, however much faster the Fw 190 was than the Stuka, it was still too slow in the face of new Soviet fighters unencumbered by drag-inducing bomb racks and additional heavy armor. A partial answer to this limitation was the Fw 190D, affectionately called "Dora" by its Luftwaffe pilots. The D model was substantially faster than its short-nosed predecessors, even if its liquid-cooled Junkers Jumo 213 engine did render it more vulnerable to ground fire. The Dora ranks as a thoroughbred among warplanes, but it was better suited to *Jagdeinsätze* (fighter operations) than to Schlachtfliegerei.

Except for the tank-killing Ju 87Gs, which remained in service in each wing's tenth squadron, the Stukas were transferred to Nachtschlacht units for night operations. In October of 1944, production of this hopelessly antiquated dive bomber finally ceased.

By June 1944, the third anniversary of Barbarossa, aviation gasoline shortages returned to stay. All reserves had been used up in anticipation of capturing Russian oil fields in the Caucasus Mountains, an expectation that proved unrealistic. The resulting severe crises precipitated a major change of strategy. Enemy tanks would no longer be attacked on sight, even those that had penetrated the lines; instead, Schlachtflieger struck only those tanks actually attacking German forces. As the German army suffered a shortage of antitank weapons, this lessening of Luftwaffe support left the Heer in bad straits.

In the summer and fall of 1944, Operation Bagration—the U.S.S.R.'s Belorussian campaign—gained momentum. Beginning in the central sector of the front, it launched a final inexorable thrust westward. By this time, the Soviet air force was numerically and qualitatively a major threat to the new Focke-Wulfs. Even the arrival of lethal hollow-load antitank rockets in October 1944 failed to make up lost ground. Each Geschwader equipped one Staffel in each of its component Gruppen with this armament for tank suppression duties. The rocket-carrying Fw 190s of these *Panzerbekämp-fungsstaffeln* (antitank squadrons) proved effective against tanks.

Interestingly, antitank rockets might have been developed and used much earlier, but Soviet use of the unsuccessful RS 82 as early as 1941 led the Germans initially to dismiss rockets as unsuitable against pinpoint targets (this despite JG 54's successes with rocket armament against shipping on Lake Ladoga early in the Siege of Leningrad). The 88-mm Panzerblitz, six of which could be carried under each wing of an Fw 190,

Rocket armament on Focke-Wulfs broke up tight formations of American bombers, rendering them more vulnerable to individual fighter attacks. This Fw 190 A-4/R6 carries one W.Gr. 21 rocket under each wing. (SI 77-12506)

Four W.Gr. 28/32 air-to-ground rocket projectiles were carried under the wings of Fw 190 F-8s. A development of the W.Gr. 21, it was not a particularly successful weapon. Courtesy of Werkefoto via Peter Petrick. (SI 86-3810)

could penetrate armor 120-mm to 140-mm thick. Soviet tanks, resistant even to the Ju 87G's 37-mm cannon, had plating only 80-mm to 90-mm thick; with these rockets, Rudel's famous attack from dead astern was no longer a necessity.

Attrition among the German ground attack units—as everywhere in the Wehrmacht of late 1944—was horrifying. It was a bleak Christmas for the survivors, many of whom wondered about families in places now under Russian occupation. The start of 1945 found the Third Reich demoralized and near collapse. Rudel, the indestructible Schlachtflieger, was still adding to his personal score, despite the recent loss of a leg to Soviet flak.[23]

"Wherever you look, masses of men and material, all Russian, mostly Mongolian," wrote Rudel. "Are their reserves of manpower so inexhaustible? We get fresh practical evidence that the productive capacity of the U.S.S.R. has been greatly underestimated by everybody and that no one knows the true facts. The masses of tanks, time and again unimaginable in number, are the most convincing proof of this."[24]

All ground attack Focke-Wulfs were extremely effective workhorses, but they came too late to make a significant difference in the course of the war. It is interesting to speculate what course Barbarossa might have taken had Fw 190s reached properly organized ground attack units using optimal tactics as early as 1942.

Extending from Bagration, a Soviet thrust late in 1944 pushed west through East Prussia, encircling Berlin the following spring. Soviet gains along the Ukranian fronts, and farther south through the Balkans, further eroded a rapidly collapsing front. The U.S.S.R.'s air and ground forces, now enjoying a decisive superiority in equipment and manpower, pressed a shrinking Germany from one side as the western Allies (after D-Day) pushed from the other; there could now be no shifts of any consequence in Germany's favor.

With the noose tightening in the spring of 1945, the Schlachtflieger had to contend with American planes as well as Soviet (being bounced by American P-51s was a particular hazard). Most planes were grounded by fuel shortages, their pilots and mechanics anxiously awaiting the inevitable

One of the SG 2 Focke-Wulfs taking part in Rudel's surrender flight was this Fw 190 A-9 Jabo. Equipped with a central bomb rack, this late-war variant lacks wing racks and features standard fighter-version 20-mm MG 151 outboard wing cannon. This photograph was taken at Kitzingen, Germany, on May 7, 1945. Courtesy of Ray Toliver. (SI 85-18831)

conclusion. It was all over by the end of April; Adolf Hitler committed suicide as Soviet forces crushed the last pockets of resistance in his former capital.

LIFE OF A SCHLACHTFLIEGER

What was it like to be a ground attack pilot in the latter half of 1944? Life at the front offered minimal facilities and little comfort. The airfield, perhaps shared with just one other squadron, was at times no more than a cleared grain field with poor drainage and wheel ruts that jolted one's teeth. If no buildings had been erected home was a tent.

Old hands knew to be ready to leave at a moment's notice; each unit was a chess piece on a vast board, lifted and set down elsewhere by unseen players far to the rear. Relocation to other bases sometimes took place just one jump ahead of Soviet tanks, whose clanking roar filled the night. The air echelon in this case would attack at dawn to cover the withdrawal of ground personnel.

In structure, Schlacht forces paralleled the *Jagd* and *Kampf* branches of the Luftwaffe. The smallest unit was the *Staffel* (similar to the American squadron), which had a nominal strength of some sixteen planes and pilots. Three (later four) Staffeln formed a *Gruppe* (comparable to a group in the U.S. Army Air Forces), the basic operational and administrative unit of the Luftwaffe. Three Gruppen—the *erste* (first), *zweite* (second), and *dritte* (third)—in turn made up the *Geschwader* (equivalent to the American wing or British group). Numbering of Staffeln was sequential; squadrons one through three formed the first group, four through six the second, and seven through nine the third. Unique to ground attack units was the

The ER 4 supplemental bomb rack increased the effectiveness of ground attack Focke-Wulfs. Supported by the ETC 501 fuselage rack, the ER 4 in turn carried up to four small bombs that could be individually dropped. Augmenting the four wing bombs, this rack gave the Fw 190 a total of eight 50-kg bombs. Courtesy of Heinz J. Nowarra. (SI 85-17520)

Focke-Wulf Fw 190G Jabos
*(fighter-bombers) entered combat
before their close cousins, the Fw
190Fs. Framed by a stockpile of
250-kg bombs is an Fw 190 G-3 of
II./SG 10. Courtesy of Gebhard Aders
via Peter Petrick. (SI 86-3837)*

presence of a tenth squadron equipped with Ju 87Gs, the last Stukas to remain in daytime service. These carried the special designation 10.Pz for *Panzerzerstörer* or "tank destroyer," one example being 10.Pz/SG 2.

Finally, Schlachtgeschwadern also had *Stab* (staff) flights of four aircraft at both wing and group levels. Command personnel often flew these "headquarters aircraft" on combat operations with the Geschwader's Staffeln. Gruppen and Geschwaderstab aircraft were also used to supplement depleted Staffeln in emergencies. Above the Geschwader level were the *Fliegerkorps* (roughly equivalent to USAAF divisions), and regional *Luftflotten* or air fleets (comparable to but smaller in scope than the individual air forces within the USAAF).

Schlachtgruppen were autonomous, fully motorized for transfers to new bases (they relied on external help only when transport aircraft were needed for shifts to distant operating theaters). Each Gruppe had its own airplane and vehicle repair facilities; communications, intelligence, and meteorological sections; armament specialists; and so on. In addition, they had light aircraft like the Fieseler Fi 156 Storch and the Focke-Wulf Fw 58 Weihe for liaison and light cargo duties.[25]

Increasingly in late 1944, replacements with little flight time reached the front because severe fuel rationing denied them adequate training. Also on hand were former bomber pilots lacking aerobatic and gunnery skills, released by the shift from offensive bombers to defensive fighters. Veterans of Stuka days, with the coveted Ritterkreuz[26] around their necks attesting to hundreds of operational missions, were now very few; it was nevertheless their capability, and that of experienced ground personnel, that kept Schlachtfliegerei alive.

It was at times difficult for the newer ground attack pilots to feel part of their groups, let alone their famous wings. The support of troops along a

*A returning SG 2 Fw 190 F-8, still
carrying its wing bombs, is guided to
its dispersal by a ground crew
member. Evidence of a substantial oil
leak shows on the cowling. Courtesy of
Peter Petrick. (SI 86-3813)*

wide front and defense against enemy aerial attack dictated an extreme dispersal of Geschwader strength. As attrition took its toll of experienced leaders, individual Staffeln operating in relative isolation were increasingly crippled by inadequate tactics and training.

In any campaign, the ground attack pilot generally went first to soften up the enemy. If ground forces were routed he came last, driven to defend the rearmost units by the desperate knowledge that hundreds—perhaps thousands—of lives depended on him. Ironically, his reward was now generally the oft-repeated accusation of cowardice from a High Command disenchanted with its Luftwaffe.

Tactics depended on the mission. According to the alert status, pilots held a specific *Einsatzbereitschaft* (operational readiness). If on two-hour alert, they could relax. If on twenty-minute alert, they stayed near their airplanes with flight gear at hand. Ground crews worked on the machines, fitting them with bombs appropriate to the types of missions slated.

When scrambled, pilots raced for their Fw 190s and started up while ground crews strapped them in. After take-off, the flight immediately formed up and flew in vee-formations. If enemy fighter defense was expected, there would be a rendezvous with escort fighters. Once over enemy territory, the *Gefechtsreihe* was adopted. This consisted of a loose line-abreast with a separation of 80 to 100 meters (270 to 330 feet); this formation provided the greatest protection from flak.

Approach course and height were chosen to avoid flak. Broken cloud cover was welcomed, for it provided the greatest degree of surprise.

"For the approach flight," states Ernst Kupfer, "5,000 meters was fully sufficient. We didn't go any higher because we couldn't see enough."[27]

Low-level flight was avoided at all costs because of the dangers of ground fire. While the Russians made limited use of radar, they lacked efficient fighter control techniques for the interception of enemy aircraft, unlike the British whose Dowding system had been so disastrous to the Luftwaffe in 1940. As a result, only nature—in the form of low ceilings and minimal visibility—forced occasional low-level operations.

"In poor visibility weather conditions," states ground attack expert Bruno Meyer, "a helpful aid to precise navigation was followed (lake regions, river beds, railroad lines, cities and villages, woods), to make the target from there on out easier to find."[28]

Ground attack Focke-Wulfs were generally "dirtier" machines than their fighter brethren, both literally and in the aerodynamic sense. Day-to-day operations from primitive airfields left little time for cleaning. Courtesy of Peter Petrick. (SI 86-3811)

A Soviet T-34/76 tank, destroyed by German aerial attack, sits abandoned in 1942. Courtesy of Uwe Feist. (SI 86-4370)

Ground attack methods depended on the targets, which might be
bridges, locomotives, troop or supply columns, ships, communication centers, ammunition dumps, or airfields. Pilots also took into account anticipated flak and fighter defense when deciding how to attack. Instead of the
Stuka's classic sixty-to-ninety-degree dive bombing assault, the Focke-
Wulfs generally employed two other methods:

First, there was a shallow dive of twenty to fifty degrees, often in
stages, starting at 2,500 to 5,000 feet above ground level and descending to
1,000 to 2,000 feet, at which point the bomb or bombs were released.

Second, where greater accuracy was required and the bomb type
permitted it, an on-the-deck attack was used. The pilot began at 300 to 1,000
feet, diving to gain speed and racing in low over the ground. For Focke-
Wulfs equipped with hollow-charge rockets, this was the way to kill a tank.
"Where possible, bombs were dropped individually or in pairs," General
Hitschhold states. "Only in the face of strong defense were bombs dropped
all at once."[29]

Attack groups at squadron strength or more would split into the
two-plane *Rotte* or the four-plane *Schwarm* during the attack (the Schwarm
was the famous finger-four formation, and could break into two leader-and-
wingman Rotten for greater flexibility in combat). If flak was a problem, the
flight would generally divide in two. One element would race for the target
while the other—slightly behind—would attack flak installations as they
opened up, as well as all smaller sources of ground fire. These Fw 190s used
bombs and internal armament in suppression duties of this type.

A similar ploy was adopted if Soviet fighters appeared on the scene.
The attacking force would split in two; one half would salvo bombs (if
necessary) and either take up station as top cover or engage the enemy,
whichever better served to protect the low element during its attack.

If the target lay near the front, the Fockes dived away over the lines
to regain altitude safely over their own territory for additional assaults. If

Another view of the Förstersonde Focke-Wulf illustrates the faired twin-barrel SG 113A installation in the left wing. Although this system was successfully tested against a captured Soviet tank, it was not used operationally. Courtesy of Heinz J. Nowarra. (SI 86-3834)

The Abwurfbehälter, *or cluster bomb, was perhaps the most effective—and inhumane—weapon of Schlachtfliegerei. A cannister that scattered small fragmentation bombs when released, it was used against personnel, supply columns, and other unarmored targets. Courtesy of Peter Petrick. (SI 86-3806)*

Carrying a 250-kg bomb, an Fw 190 D-12 takes off from a rainy eastern front airfield early in 1945. Courtesy of Peter Petrick. (SI 86-3800)

not, pilots made use of woods and lakes as zones of comparative safety to begin their climb-out (the moment of greatest vulnerability).

Briefings before each flight were as thorough as possible; pilots were given directions and flight times from known landmarks to help them locate even the most heavily camouflaged targets. To fly to the combat area, they used maps of up to 1:1,000,000 scale; when in the target area itself, they used much more detailed maps of 1:100,000 or 1:300,000 scale, as well as photographs and diagrams provided during briefing.

Ground forces used various means to identify desired aerial support. These included target marker panels, smoke bombs, and so on. Even without the direct radio link that Kupfer wanted, signals existed whereby the direction and range of targets across the front lines could be communicated to the supporting aircraft.

One especially effective measure was the placement of a pilot officer on the front lines or in the command vehicle of a tank assault force, with a special radio link to his comrades by which he could call in accurate air support. A variation on this system, also performed on a limited basis during the war, was to have him coordinate air strikes from a Fieseler Storch, much as forward air controllers would do in Vietnam decades later. In view of the success of these special measures, it is difficult to understand why such close cooperation was the exception rather than the rule.

The flight leader in any operation directed his unit by radio. Little communication was necessary, as all missions were thoroughly discussed on the ground before take-off. Code words—usually multisyllabic for maximal intelligibility—were used to convey orders quickly. They were not designed to fool the Soviets (anything overheard could not be acted upon in time in any event), and were not regularly changed. (See appendix 5 for ground attack radio terminology.)

It may be seen that the demands upon ground attack pilots were extraordinary. For this reason, the ranks of Schlachtfliegerei were traditionally filled by pilots who in basic flight instruction showed the highest levels of skill. They were sent to *Schlachtfliegerschul-Geschwadern* (ground attack training wings), where they flew front-line aircraft and learned formation flying, bombing, aerial gunnery, aerial combat, and advanced navigation. Their studies included army and navy tactics and cooperation with these forces. Passing students then reported to the *Ergänzungsstaffeln* (replacement squadrons) for their first exposure to combat.

Those showing special aptitudes and promise received yet more training and became Panzerschlacht pilots. Once they mastered heavy-cannon gunnery and rocket firing, they graduated to arguably the most dangerous work in the Luftwaffe; the head-on low-altitude killing of Soviet tanks.

Schlacht means slaughter. From the start of Barbarossa to the end of the war, the term remained particularly apt.

3

Flying the Fw 190

THE GERMAN PERSPECTIVE

Fw 190 F-8s of an unidentified ground attack unit prepare to take off with 250-kg cluster bombs under their fuselages. The flatness of the vast eastern front is readily evident. Courtesy of Heinz J. Nowarra. (SI 86-3838)

Evaluation of any aircraft type is best left to those who flew it. Dr. Heinz Lange pursued a distinguished law career in the postwar era, but during World War II he was a fighter pilot on the Russian front. He writes:

I first flew the Focke-Wulf Fw 190 on November 8, 1942, at Vyasma in the Soviet Union. I was absolutely thrilled. We flew it until the beginning of May 1945, except for an extended period in 1944–45 during which my unit again operated Me 109s (I believe because Fw 190 production initially fell short of home defense needs). I flew every fighter version of the Fw 190 employed on the eastern front, including the D-9 right at the end. Because of its smaller fuselage, visibility was somewhat better out of the Me 109. In most respects, however, vision out of all three was equally excellent. I believe the Focke-Wulf was more maneuverable than the Messerschmitt; although the latter could make a tighter horizontal turn, if you mastered the Fw 190 you could pull a lot of G's and do just about as well. In terms of control force and feel the 109 was heavier on the stick, but all three were nice to fly. Aerobatics were a pleasure!

Structurally, the Focke was distinctly superior to the Messerschmitt, especially in dives. The radial engine of the Fw 190A was also more resistant to enemy fire. Firepower, which varied with the particular series, was fairly even in all German fighters. The central cannon of the Messerschmitt was naturally more accurate; that was really a meaningful advantage only in fighter-to-fighter combat, however. The 109's 30-mm cannon frequently jammed, especially in hard turns—I lost at least six confirmed kills this way. Our other on-board weapons were reliable, accurate, and effective.

Its small landing gear made the Me 109 very sensitive to crosswinds and uneven ground on takeoff and landing. We had unbelievably high aircraft losses and personal injuries in this way. In contrast, the landing gear of the Focke was stable. When taxiing, visibility forward was worse out of the 190 than the 109, but that was easily solved by S-turning. Visibility was also worse out of the 190 during takeoff and landing because these were performed in a tail-low attitude, unlike the 109 which was fairly level at these times. A dangerous characteristic of the Focke-Wulf was that in very tight high-G turns it would sometimes, suddenly and with no warning, whip into a turn in the opposite direction. In a dogfight or near the ground, this could have a very bad result. The Messerschmitt had leading edge slots that hindered this type of stall.

In the development of our fighter operations, the most significant step was our transition from the closed Kette of three planes to the four-plane "finger-four" Schwarm. This innovation was developed during the Spanish Civil War with considerable help by Werner Mölders, and was also adopted by most other countries during World War II. In great measure I attribute to this tactic the high number of victories attained by German fighter pilots.

After just a few flights in the Focke-Wulf, I had to break off a mission because of engine trouble and return to our own lines for an emergency landing. The belly landing was no problem and illustrated the sturdiness of the plane; there was almost no damage except for the propeller. I never had any more engine failures, nor did I ever have to parachute from a plane. I did come

This Fw 190 D-9 of II./JG 2 was caught in a frame taken by the automatic strike camera of a Martin B-26 Marauder. Skimming between the B-26 bomber and its falling 500-lb bombs, the feared Dora—arguably the best Luftwaffe fighter operational in World War II—passes breathtakingly close to its prey. Courtesy of USAF. (SI 71-112-3)

Oberleutnant Fritz Seyffardt, Knight's Cross holder and thirty-victory ace, joined II./SG 2 on the Black Sea in 1943. Almost all his victories were against Ilyushin Shturmoviks, heavily armored Soviet ground attack machines known to be extremely difficult to shoot down. Courtesy of Fritz Seyffardt. (SI 85-15646)

back many times with damage from aerial combat and ground fire, but my Focke always brought me back for a normal landing.

My opinion of the Me 109G, Fw 190A, and Fw 190 D-9—all of which I flew willingly, is that they were superb aircraft for their day in terms of performance and reliability. I can say that for me my first choice of aircraft was the Fw 190 D-9 and my second the A; the Me 109 ranks third.[1]

The vast majority of Focke-Wulfs served in regular fighter operations; far fewer Fw 190s were employed in the ground attack role, where substantially different equipment and tactics came into play. Fritz Seyffardt, a young pilot in SG 2 Immelmann, rapidly learned what it was like to be a Schlachtflieger:

I joined the second Gruppe in 1943 at Anapa on the Black Sea. From there we moved to a grass field at Varvarovka, southwest of Kharkov, which became our base for taking part in the great Kursk offensive. In the following months we remained in the southern sector, flying from various fields behind the front lines. Later on we participated in operations in Sevastopol in the Crimea until the end of fighting there, then to Romania for operations on the Jassy front. From there I was transferred back home as an instructor of young pilots. The group commander during my tenure was Major Heinz Frank, who later died. Rudel commanded the wing.

In 1942, I saw and flew my first Focke-Wulf Fw 190; I was thrilled with this machine. During the war I flew the Fw 190A, F, and G models, and also the Messerschmitt Bf 109F. The Messerschmitts (all versions) didn't appeal to me because they were dangerous in dives (wing failure), and on take-off and landing because of their narrow landing gear. As for the Focke-Wulf Fw 190D, I only flew it once. Thanks to the more powerful engine its performance was considerably improved, especially at altitude.

The difference between the Fw 190 and the Bf 109 was that there was more room in the Focke-Wulf's cockpit and the controls were simpler—for example, landing flaps and trim were electric. Another pronounced difference was the stability of the Fw 190. Thanks to its through-wing spars and wide landing gear the machine was substantially more stable and robust in flight, and especially in landing on rough fields.

Visibility was better in flight than with the Bf 109, though worse on take-off and landing because of the Focke's three-point attitude. At great height, engine performance was inadequate. Otherwise the machine was pleasant to fly and had for the most part no critical or dangerous character-

Armament hatches and cowling open, Fw 190 KS+ME receives maintenance on an open field. Although a rack is not fitted to this Fw 190 A-6, the piled bombs in the foreground and the attachment lugs under the fuselage suggest that there is provision for one to be fitted. On the ground near the aircraft's tire is the 20-mm MG 151 removed from the right wing. (SI 83-14514)

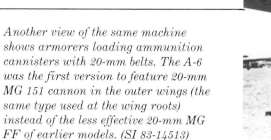

Another view of the same machine shows armorers loading ammunition cannisters with 20-mm belts. The A-6 was the first version to feature 20-mm MG 151 cannon in the outer wings (the same type used at the wing roots) instead of the less effective 20-mm MG FF of earlier models. (SI 83-14513)

istics. Normal range of our F models was approximately 600–700 kilometers (375–425 miles). The average mission on the Russian front lasted 45–60 minutes.

Firepower was very good. As a rule we had two 20-mm cannon and two machine guns. There was also provision for the installation of an additional two 20-mm cannon in the outer wing panels. As a flying tactic, we had the greatest success when we flew open, in other words aproximately 80 to 100 meters separation from airplane to airplane. In the target area we split into the small two-plane Rotte elements for the attack, only reassembling into larger formations on the return flight.

In altogether about five hundred front-line missions, I had to make several belly landings on differing terrains, something that could be done without undue difficulty. Once I had to bail out right over Sevastopol as my machine had been shot down in flames. The radial engine was quite subject to improper cooling of the rear cylinders, which led in my career to two or three engine failures, and the resultant belly landings.

As a Schlachtflieger, I had less to do with enemy fighters than with enemy ground attack machines, of which I shot down thirty. We also had contact with Russian fighters, but they for the most part avoided us so we really had no problem with them. I encountered British and American fighters only at the end of the war; we felt the English Spitfire was the more dangerous machine for us because of its superiority at high altitudes.[2]

Fritz Seyffardt jumps from the wing of his Focke-Wulf. Seyffardt first flew the Fw 190 during training in 1942 and was thrilled with the machine. Courtesy of Fritz Seyffardt. (SI 85-15645)

It was extremely difficult to become an ace in Schlachtfliegerei because ground attack Focke-Wulfs were heavier, less maneuverable, slower, and less heavily armed than their fighter counterparts. Fritz Seyffardt's remarkable success against the legendary Ilyushin IL-2 Shturmovik—a plane so heavily armored as to be almost impossible to shoot down—earned him a Ritterkreuz, but not the fame accorded the more glamorous fighter pilots.

Feldwebel Peter Traubel, a young noncommissioned officer, flew with the earlier Schlachtgeschwader 2 (before the Immelmann wing took this designation),[3] and after the reorganization of late 1943 with SG 4. His combat flying took place in Russia and—in the face of Soviet advances late the following year—in Hungary.

> During the war I fulfilled my duties as a Luftwaffe pilot. In September 1943 I joined SG 2. My commanding officer in the III. Gruppe was a Hauptmann Dornbreck. There I flew an Fw 190F.
>
> The Fw 190 as an airplane was very advanced. The wide landing gear gave better tracking stability than with the Messerschmitt Bf 109. There were no unnecessary controls in the Focke-Wulf. The pilot's seat was comfortable, and armor protection was adequate. Instruments were easily scanned, a fact which pleased me on my first flight in the 190. I found myself very quickly at home.
>
> During combat we feared the great risk of fire from being hit. I remember that a fellow pilot burned in his cockpit when he was hit in the fuel system. The inside of his plane instantly burst into flames.
>
> Our heavy loading was also a problem. The Fw 190 was very cumbersome at full gross weight. I would never have traded it for another airplane, nevertheless, and today still regard it in form and performance as a magnificent machine.
>
> I had the chance to inspect a Soviet fighter once that had been bellied in. . . . These Russian airplanes were primitively equipped, but in the air were an enemy to be taken seriously. In turns they were the equal of the Fw 190, if not even more maneuverable. When they appeared, we'd drop our external loads as otherwise we would have been sitting ducks for the Russians.
>
> Even without enemy aircraft, there was a dangerous enemy to be feared. This was the ground defense. I recall a day when four of us flew an attack against a column of replacements. All three of my colleagues were brought down by flak. We never learned their fate.
>
> Despite these hindrances, we inflicted telling ground attacks on the enemy. In March 1945 I flew my last mission. After that we were transferred to the ground forces because of a shortage of fuel. I was captured by the Russians outside of Vienna. What became of my Kameraden, I don't know; neither in prison nor subsequently have I had any contact with former members of the SG.[4]

This Fw 190A will soon be counted a confirmed victory for an Allied fighter pilot. This frame from gun camera footage shows the stricken plane with its left main landing gear down—the result of battle damage—and canopy jettisoned to enable the pilot to parachute to safety. Courtesy of USAF. (SI 86-3827)

Another Fw 190A receives hits on the right wing as its pilot pulls it into a high-G turn past the vertical. This dogfight ensued when the Luftwaffe fighter was intercepted by a P-51 while attacking American heavy bombers over Germany. Courtesy of National Archives. (SI 86-3816)

The last thing many Allied fighter pilots saw before being shot down was this view of an Fw 190 coming straight on. The fighter's minimal frontal area is apparent. Courtesy of National Archives. (SI 86-6434)

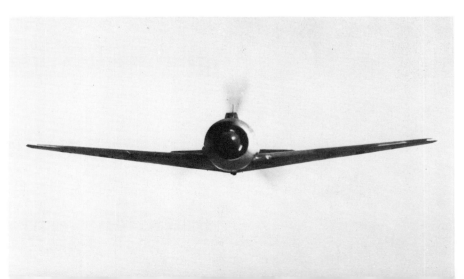

Ground attack pilot Karl Stein poses in the cockpit of his Focke-Wulf. Attached to SG 1, Stein flew Ju 87s and Fw 190s along the northern and central sectors of the eastern front during World War II. Courtesy of Karl Stein via John Bessette. (SI 85-14224)

A Jabo-Rei, or long-range fighter-bomber, this Fw 190 A-5/U13 had its range greatly extended with two aerodynamically clean wing drop tanks. Courtesy of Werkefoto via Peter Petrick. (SI 86-3823)

Karl Stein joined Schlachtgeschwader 1 late in 1943. His erste Gruppe (I./SG 1), which before the reorganization belonged to Stukageschwader 5, still operated Ju 87s, although the dritte Gruppe (III./SG 1) already had Fw 190s. The following year, when Soviet Havocs (American A-20 bombers received under Lend-Lease) destroyed almost all their Stukas, he and other I./SG 1 pilots felt that they must now get Focke-Wulfs; to their disappointment they received instead the zweite Gruppe's Ju 87s because II./SG 1 was getting Focke-Wulfs. It was not until January 1945 that his Gruppe's turn came to receive factory-fresh Fockes.

"We were very pleased with the Fw 190," he states, remembering the easy transition. "It was very friendly to the pilot."[5]

Stein's personal Focke-Wulf was *Schwarze 2* (planes were referred to by their identifying fuselage number, in this case a black 2). He picked it up in the Breslau area of Silesia (now Wroclaw, Poland) and put it to hard use along the Oder River, where some thirty bridges had to be destroyed to impede advancing Soviet troops. Although fighter opposition was not as strong as it was in the south—where SG 2 operated—Stein had many occasions to observe enemy aircraft close at hand.

"Our thought was that they have beautiful airplanes but they do not know how to fly them," he says. "They just made one pass—if they attacked us at all—and were gone. They always fired from much too far away, and were hopeless at deflection shooting. They could climb much faster than we, whereas we could outdive them. They could also outturn us. Almost always they would just throw on power and pull back on the stick."[6]

Stein recalls one encounter when two fighters were on the tail of a Focke-Wulf. "I slipped in between the two of them and fired on the leader. He turned and I followed. Then he did a stupid thing, something you never do in a dog fight—he reversed direction. I missed him but he turned again and I got him. His wingman never fired at me; perhaps he was afraid of hitting his leader."[7]

Better still than the radial-engined Lavochkins and the sharp-nosed Yaks, Karl Stein knew the Ilyushin IL-2s. In his Stuka days, returning from a mission, he would often pass Shturmoviks going the opposite direction after attacking German targets. Despite their enmity, there existed a strange empathy with the Soviet ground attack forces that often prompted the Germans to wave. Once they had their Focke-Wulfs, however, it was a different story.

"The infantry suffered heavily from IL-2 attacks," he remembers, "so we were anxious to get them. I apparently got the rear gunner of one because his gun pointed upwards, and I expended all my ammunition—guns and cannon—on the plane. He started smoking, his right landing gear dropped, and he slowed way down. But I couldn't knock him down. When I broke off, he was still in the air though he probably didn't make it back to base."[8]

The Shturmoviks were tough—Stein recalls seeing 20-mm flak bounce right off one—but at times suffered from ineffective pilot tactics. Stein notes that they struck columns at right angles, preferring a single quick hit to the more dangerous and effective lengthwise attacks that the Germans pressed home. The Ilyushins bombed airfields in mass flights, dropping together and turning for home, whereas their German counterparts would break into two-plane elements and attack specific targets on the airfield in multiple passes. Stein dismisses Soviet ground attack tactics as inept.

Interestingly, Soviet fighters were more adaptable. They quickly adopted the finger-four formation, the passing of enemy aircraft to attack

Another Jabo-Rei version of the standard Focke-Wulf fighter, this Fw 190 A-4/U8 begins its take-off roll in 1943. Under the fuselage, it carries four 50-kg bombs on an ER 4 multiple bomb adapter. (SI 86-3797)

from the rear, and other proven Luftwaffe tactics. Their limitation was rather one of quality; Stein and his colleagues felt that Soviet pilots rarely realized the potential of their excellent machines, a failure they attribute primarily to poor pilot training.

A fundamental conceptual difference shaped the Soviet air force. This was the extreme priority accorded artillery, including antiaircraft guns, which left the air force as little more than an adjunct to be employed where guns couldn't reach. Soviet flak was devastating, but fighters showed little commitment to exercising air superiority.

"Even when we knew they had the fighters," Stein observes, "they would not be up in the air. You could fly in peace for one or two hours before they appeared."[9]

In fact, Soviet appreciation of the vast scale of their theater led to a conscious decision not to assert air superiority as the term was understood in other theaters of the war. They allowed the Luftwaffe relative freedom of action, choosing instead to conserve resources for specific operations. It was also true that Soviet fighter opposition was substantially less intense in the north; if Karl Stein found Soviet fighters unwilling to engage in combat, his fellow Schlachtflieger in the "hotter" southern stretches of the long front found the opposite to be true from 1943 on.

On April 20, 1945, Hitler's fifty-sixth and last birthday, Stein was in a flight of ten Focke-Wulfs that engaged forty Yaks. There was not a trace of hesitation among the German pilots, he remembers, all of whom were young and eager. In the end, three of the Yaks fell northeast of Berlin while no Fw 190s were lost.

English and American aircraft appeared on the scene in these closing days of the European war. Spitfires were the most feared, then Mustangs,

Every Focke-Wulf production series had a variety of subtypes, the multirole capabilities of which serve to confuse the always nebulous distinctions between fighter, fighter-bomber, ground attack machine, bomber killer, and so forth. Here an Fw 190 A-5 fighter is configured with bomb rack and deleted outboard wing armament for ground support duties. Courtesy of Archiv Redemann. (SI 86-3796)

and even the Thunderbolt—the only fighter able to outdive a Focke-Wulf—was held in respectful regard. The primary reason was that American and British pilot training was known to be excellent.

"We were fighter-bombers, not fighters," Stein states. "We had the confidence to dogfight with the Russians, but we would never have taken on the Allies. Never!"[10]

Stein tells one story of the toll taken by attrition in flying personnel. A particularly limited pilot who had flown hundreds of missions in Heinkel He 111s was transferred into I./SG 1 and flew with them on a mission to Oranienburg on April 18, 1945. With strict radio silence being observed, Stein and others tried the entire time by hand signals to tell him that he had left his landing gear down, but he never understood. The bomber pilot flew the entire mission—doubtlessly at much higher throttle settings—with his wheels down!

Karl Stein placed great stock in the ruggedness of the Focke-Wulf. Belly landings in the F and G models, for example, were no problem and the machines were quickly put back into the air. "Many pilots made better landings on the ETC bomb rack than they did on wheels," he asserts with a smile.[11]

Stein, who flew jets in the postwar era, is almost reverential in his appreciation of his wartime mount; he considers the Fw 190 one of the best and most versatile single-seat combat aircraft ever built. In great measure, he attributes his survival in the dangerous business of Schlachtfliegerei to the Fw 190.

Ground personnel remove the cowling cover and pull the propeller through before starting an Fw 190 A-9 of 2./JG 11. This plane, engaged in a last-ditch effort to check the Soviet advance into Berlin in April 1945, was photographed at Strausberg, just east of the Reich's capital. Courtesy of Peter Petrick. (SI 86-3803)

Such enthusiasm is shared by non-German pilots who flew the Focke-Wulf in combat. Janos (today John) Jarmy flew Fw 190 A-6s and A-8s in an all-Hungarian unit during the latter part of World War II. Following Ju 87 training he served in Poland, on the northern part of the Russian front, and in his homeland. His two aerial victories were a Russian Airacobra (the American P-39) and an IL-2 Shturmovik.

"It was a fantastic machine," he states of the Fw 190, "a very, very good airplane! It was much better than the Messerschmitt—I'd take it anytime over the Bf 109."[12]

Hans Ulrich Rudel logged time in Fw 190s, a fact often overshadowed by his Stuka exploits. His introduction came in June 1944 when he checked himself out on the first examples received by the Geschwaderstab of SG 2. "I finish up my self-training," he writes in his book *Stuka Pilot*, "by going out straight away on one or two sorties in the frontal area with the new type and feel quite safe in it."[13]

In the coming months Rudel had a number of exciting experiences in his new plane. Mustangs destroyed an Fw 190 he was landing, but he escaped death by climbing out and dropping to the ground while his doomed plane was still rolling. On another occasion Soviet 40-mm flak blew off his canopy; he suddenly found himself, utterly unscratched, flying an open-cockpit airplane! Another time engine damage forced him to break off pursuit of La-5 and Yak-9 fighters and make a belly landing. Even after jettisoning the hood he couldn't see ahead because of smoke and heavy oil on the windscreen; a church steeple whizzed by, narrowly missing his wings, but the landing was successful.

Oberst Hans Ulrich Rudel, the most experienced ground attack pilot of all, was the last commander of SG 2. Here he sits between subordinate commanders Schwirblatt and Kennel, on the occasion of the Immelmann wing's surrender to American forces at Kitzingen, Germany, on May 7, 1945. Courtesy of Ray Toliver. (SI 85-18830)

Retired Generalleutnant Adolf Galland, General der Jagdflieger until he fell out of favor with the German High Command, enjoyed the best vantage from which to place the Focke-Wulf Fw 190 in a balanced context. The following are his personal views:

It was indeed a great fighter plane. Initially during the introduction of the first Fw 190 A-1s, there were many technical problems, most centering on the cooling of the engine. The design of the BMW 801 C2 and D2 engines was very advanced, all functions being controlled by a very sensitive automatic device called the Kommandogerät.

By the end of 1941 the fighter plane became operational with my II./JG 26 "Schlageter." The pilots liked the Fw 190 very much as far as handling, performance, and armament were concerned. Compared with the Me 109 series of the time, the Fw 190 was superior, but this did not hold true in altitudes above 8,000 meters (25,000 feet). Especially against bombers the Fw 190 was by far superior because of its heavier armament, its lower vulnerability, and its better protection for the pilot. All these features were favorable for fighter bomber and Schlachtflieger operations. The potential for carrying up to 1,000 kilograms of bombs, combined with excellent take-off and landing characteristics, favored use of the Fw 190 in nearly all other roles as well as fighter. In total, 19,999 Fw 190s were built, 13,365 as fighters and 6,634 as fighter-bombers and Schlachtflieger aircraft.

Although ground attack played its greatest role in the east, it was also important in the west after D-Day. This Fw 190 F-8 was photographed on a paved dispersal in Avord, France, southeast of Bourges. Courtesy of Peter Petrick. (SI 85-18823)

Fw 190s with Ju 213 liquid-cooled engines were somewhat superior to those powered by the BMW 801. The long-nosed Ta 152, however, was far superior. I personally as General der Jagdflieger flew my staff Fw 190Ds. Even though I was not allowed to fly in combat, I was able to shoot down several dispersed American four-engine bombers.

Taking off in 1943 from Berlin-Staaken for a flight to Arnheim, I lost the left tire of my Fw 190. Instead of making a belly landing in Holland, I tried to make a safe landing on one wheel, which resulted in a complete crash but me healthy in the ruins.[14]

THE ALLIED PERSPECTIVE

Pilot Officer Jackson B. Mahon shared the excitement that ran through the Royal Air Force's Eagle Squadrons. In March 1942, just weeks after the battle cruisers *Scharnhorst* and *Gneisenau* ran the gantlet of the English Channel, a fellow American had shot down a strange new fighter. It wasn't the in-line engined Heinkel that they had been briefed to expect, and it certainly wasn't the too familiar Messerschmitt; this machine had the short blunt nose of a tightly cowled radial power plant. Some thought it might be an ex-French Curtiss 75 Hawk. Word soon circulated that it was something brand new called the Fw 190.

Barry Mahon shot down two Focke-Wulfs in quick succession in April 1942, and the following month he got two more. The handsome young Californian, whose Supermarine Spitfire Mark VB AV-J carried his first name with typical American informality, now led his squadron in victories.

Pilot Officer Barry Mahon, an American ace serving with one of the RAF's Eagle Squadrons, shot down four Fw 190s and one Bf 109 before being himself shot down by an Fw 190 over Dieppe on August 19, 1942. Despite two escapes, Mahon spent the rest of the war as a German POW. Courtesy of Barry Mahon. (SI 85-18836)

"I was never terribly impressed with the airplane," he recalls of the Focke-Wulf, "but you know that a young fighter pilot can't let himself get impressed or he chickens out. So you had to believe they were no good and you convinced yourself of that."[15]

On one patrol he attacked twenty-five of the machines by himself. He was leading A Flight and reported bandits below, but the wing commander said they were Spitfires; Mahon went down anyway and found himself all alone, going so fast he shot through the German formation with time for only one shot. It wasn't enough to add to his score. Because the Fw 190 could outclimb his Spitfire VB, he rolled for the deck and raced for home at war emergency power.

Barry Mahon got his next two victories while escorting RAF Bostons on an attack on the Luftwaffe airfield at Abbeville, home of the infamous Abbeville Boys from JG 26. Among their yellow-nosed Fw 190s, Mahon saw a Bf 109 and shot it down. Killed in the encounter was fifty-two-victory ace Major Rudolf Flanz who, like so many of the Luftwaffe's old hands, retained his trusty Messerschmitt rather than switching to the newer Focke-Wulf.

On August 19, 1942, Mahon led a fighter sweep in support of the bloody and abortive Dieppe Raid. He had just become an ace by shooting down an Fw 190, and was on the tail of a sixth, when his guns went silent. At that time he estimates that there were some eighty German planes within a square mile. He broke off to return to England and rearm, but was attacked by his erstwhile prey who was angry at having lost his wingman.

One of America's earliest World War II aces (four of whose victories were Fw 190s), Barry Mahon was in turn shot down by a Focke-Wulf fighter. He jettisoned the canopy of AV-J (one of 106 RAF aircraft lost that day) and bailed out scarcely seven hundred feet up, ending up in a dinghy in the Channel to watch, enthralled, as spectacularly dramatic fighting continued overhead.

Captured by the Germans, Mahon was taken to a satellite field of JG 26, the Abbeville wing, where he was permitted to sit in the cockpit of an Fw 190. "It was terrible," remembers the Spitfire pilot, "uncomfortable and badly laid out. Things weren't where they were supposed to be and you couldn't see out."[16]

These objections notwithstanding, he urged his captors to let him take it "around the pattern" a few times. The Germans wisely decided that the honor system might fail in the face of temptation, and denied him a dash for home. Barry Mahon spent the rest of the war as a *Kriegie*[17] despite two unsuccessful escapes. He returned to California in the postwar years where—in the tradition of Escadrille Lafayette flier William Wellman—he pursued a successful career as a movie producer.

Obtaining a Focke-Wulf fighter for evaluation was an urgent priority for the RAF, whose losses had risen to insupportable levels with the appearance of the new type.[18] Seven weeks before Barry Mahon was shot down, the opportunity came when JG 2 "Richthofen" pilot Arnim Faber became disoriented and landed at Pembrey, an RAF field near Swansea, thinking it was a German field on the Cherbourg Peninsula. At dusk, he barrel-rolled over the field, lowering his gear while still inverted, and rolled out into a hot fighter pilot landing. By the time he realized his mistake, it was too late; the RAF now had an Fw 190 A-3. More Focke-Wulfs fell into British hands as the summer wore on.

Eric Brown, the Royal Navy test pilot whose experience flying captured aircraft is without parallel, was one of the pilots performing later flight evaluations. His findings, recounted in *Wings of the Luftwaffe,* were

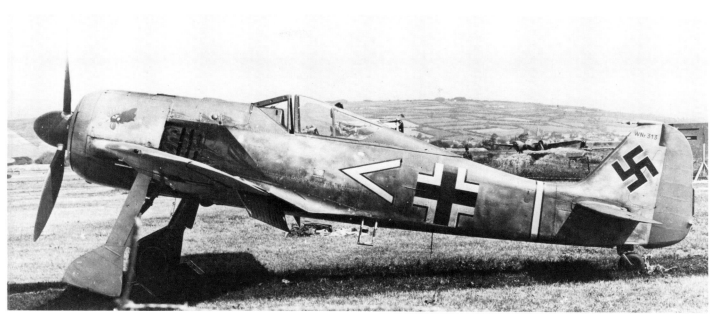

Accidentally landed at RAF Pembrey by Oberleutnant Arnim Faber on June 23, 1942, Fw 190 A-3 W.-Nr. 5313 was the first Focke-Wulf fighter to fall into Allied hands. It was extensively tested by British pilots anxious to determine its relative strengths and weaknesses. (SI A 48623-G)

that it was indeed a formidable warplane. He was tremendously impressed with it on almost all counts, noting in particular the excellent visibility and superb control harmony.

"I clearly recall the excitement with which I first examined the Focke-Wulf fighter; the impression of elegant lethality that its functional yet pleasing lines exuded," he writes. "To me it represented the very quintessence of aeronautical pulchritude from any angle."[19]

Brown's enthusiasm grew as he got to know the Focke-Wulf from a pilot's standpoint. "A good dogfighter *and* a good gun platform," he notes appreciatively, "called for just the characteristics that this fighter possessed in all important matters of stability and control."[20]

His and other tests confirmed that the Spitfire VB's only advantage lay in its tighter turn. The Fw 190's vulnerability while pulling out of dives was recognized, as were its sharp stall characteristics. Spitfire pilots were strongly encouraged to try forcing their foes into horizontal engagements, both to turn within them and, if possible, to induce the accelerated stall and opposite snap to which the Fw 190 was prone. Above all, pilots were advised to avoid dogfights in the vertical plane where Focke-Wulfs had the advantage. Later in 1942 the introduction of the Spitfire Mark IX helped shift the equation back in the British favor, but only until the Luftwaffe's improved Fw 190 A-4 appeared.

The same aircraft, sporting RAF markings and serial MP499, is inspected by an RAF pilot at Duxford in July 1942 where it was evaluated by the Air Fighting Development Unit (AFDU). (SI 86-591)

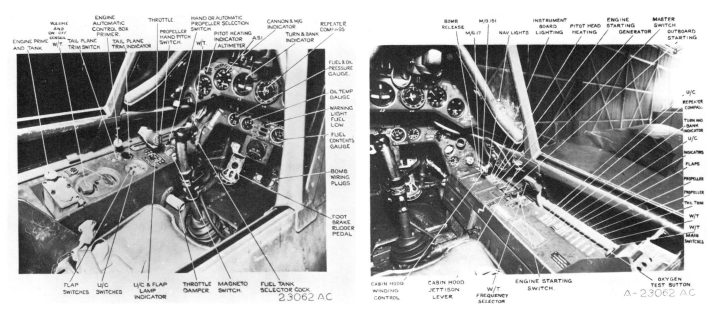

Two photographs illustrate the cockpit of Arnim Faber's Fw 190. "UC" in the captioning stands for undercarriage, the British term for landing gear. (SI 86-6432 & 86-6433)

Fw 190 A-4 PE882 was the second Focke-Wulf to fall into British hands. This machine landed accidentally at RAF West Malling on April 17, 1943. (SI 86-589)

The United States, just gearing up for strategic bombing from English bases, also had a tremendous stake in the effectiveness of Germany's new fighter. With Royal Air Force cooperation, the U.S. Army Air Forces undertook their own evaluation of a captured Focke-Wulf Fw 190A in July 1942, flying it against an RAF Mustang 1A. This American-built fighter was the Allison-engined progenitor of the Merlin-powered North American P-51s that earned fame as long-range escort fighters later in the war.

Comparison of Fw 190 with Mustang 1A: Fw 190 is approximately 2 miles an hour faster than the Mustang from sea level to 5,000 feet.

Altitude from 5,000 to 15,000 feet: Mustang 1A is faster than the 190, approximately 5 to 15 mph above 15,000 feet.

General maneuverability, climb and speed: The Fw 190 is slightly superior to the Mustang. In general under all conditions, flight of the Fw 190 is slightly better than that of the Mustang. In one instance between combat of Fw 190 and Mustang, when the Mustang attacked the Fw 190, it was found that the 190 could evade by using its superiority in the [vertical] plane then fall out in a resultant dive into a steep climb which left the Mustang behind. If the Mustang is not seen until it is fairly close it will get a chance of a short burst before it is outclimbed. Against the 190, the worst heights for the Mustang 1A were above 20,000 feet and below 3,000 feet. Endurance and climb of the Fw 190 under operational conditions including combat and climb to 25,000 feet is approximately one hour and twenty minutes of fuel. Climb to 18,000 feet maximum conditions at 165 mph is 3,000 feet to 3,250 feet per minute. Pull-up from level flight at best cruising speed is extremely high and the angle very steep. Pull-up after a dive is phenomenal.

Dive: Has a high rate of dive, and the initial acceleration is excellent. No alteration of the trim tabs is necessary going from level flight or abruptly to dive or recovery from a dive to straight and level again. This is due to a very light control. The fuel injection system allows very quick push-over without the engine quitting.

Absolute ceiling of the Fw 190 is 38,000 feet.[21]

In aerial combat, pilots inevitably formed their own opinions of the Focke-Wulf. Captain Jack Ilfrey flew Lockheed P-38 Lightnings with the 1st Fighter Group's famous 94th "Hat-in-the-Ring" Fighter Squadron in North Africa. Himself the son of a fighter pilot, Ilfrey was a skilled and colorful flier whose aircraft sported names like *The Texas Terror* and *Happy Jack's Go-Buggy*. Around the middle of December 1942, Jack saw Focke-Wulfs attacking a crippled American B-17 bomber far below. With the advantage of height, he and his squadron mates dove on the German fighters and downed several, while one of his friends was in turn shot down.

"Just as this was taking place," he writes, "[Lieutenant] Bob Neale, who was near me, yelled there were two coming in on me. I evaded the attack as quickly as possible and in the ensuing dogfight Bob Neale's and my P-38s outperformed the two Focke-Wulfs, and we were able to down both of the Jerries and confirm each other's victories. Then Neale and I teamed up to get the hell out of there because there were many more Focke-Wulfs than we had anticipated."[22]

The entire combat, during which Jack Ilfrey downed two Fw 190s, took less than five minutes. Not long afterward he had quite a different view of the enemy fighter, one denied most Allied pilots.

"There were several Fw 190s left at Youks Les Baines, Algeria, when the Germans made a hasty retreat," he recalls. "We pilots were told definitely to leave 'em alone, but being curious types we began toying with one. One of the enlisted men who helped get it fixed up was a German-speaking master sergeant; he instructed me on the instruments and placed adhesive tape with English captions by several of them. On a dare from my buddy pilots, I took it off, played around for a while, and returned. It was a very nice machine to fly. Needless to say, I was in trouble with my CO and other higher-ups. Got into a lot more when I did the same thing with an Me 109 at Biskra."[23]

After six victories in North Africa, he flew a second tour with the 20th Fighter Group in England (which soon converted to P-51s) where he ran his score up to eight. Like so many aggressive young fighter pilots, he had unquestioning faith in the superiority of his aircraft. "We had no apprehensions whatsoever," he explains. "We were damn good P-38 and P-51 pilots and nothing would keep us from getting involved with a German airplane."[24]

Lockheed P-38 ace Richard J. Lee was another "Hat-in-the-Ring" veteran who upheld the traditions of Eddie Rickenbacker's 94th Squadron from World War I. His previous victories having been Messerschmitt Bf 109s, he was anxious to appraise Germany's other first-line fighter. While accompanying Consolidated B-24 Liberators across the Mediterranean on August 9, 1943, he had his chance.

> When escorting we "essed" back and forth across the bomber formation for their protection. The B-24s always flew a very spread-out formation, never tight like the '17s, '25s, or '26s. Approximately fifteen German fighters appeared on the opposite side of the bomber formation, approaching from the 4:30 position and above us. My squadron was nearest the exposed side. We were already in a right turn so we steepened it, and my flight was on the right side of the vee formation which put us nearest the attacking fighters. Often the Germans, in my experience, did not want to risk a head-on attack with our P-38s, undoubtedly because of our concentrated firepower, so several of them—a mixed bunch of Me 109s and Fw 190s—decided a split-S was the right maneuver. One Focke-Wulf apparently decided he wanted a B-24, and may not have seen our flight. I was probably 1,000 yards off abeam his left wing, closing rapidly with my throttles to the fire wall; it simply required a hard turn to the left, beginning to fire with about a twenty-degree deflection. He blew up before he was in firing range of the bombers.[25]

This and other encounters led him to believe that the Fw 190 was a less formidable foe than the Bf 109. A great truism in evaluating fighter

In the latter years of World War II, Reichsverteidigung *(home defense) took priority over other uses of the* Focke-Wulf. *The red rear fuselage band of this* Fw 190 A-8/R8 *of II./JG 300, W.-Nr. 172 733, denotes its employment in this role. Flown by* Unteroffizier *Ernst Schröder in operations against American heavy bombers, this aircraft was damaged in a dogfight with P-51 escort fighters on November 27, 1944, and was scrapped after bellying in at Köthen, Germany. Courtesy of Ernst Schröder via Peter Petrick. (SI 85-15388)*

aircraft, however, is that any plane is only as good as its pilot, and Lee (an ace by war's end) suspected that inadequate training of younger Luftwaffe pilots might be a factor.

"I did not seem to have very many encounters with the Fw 190," Lee states. "Either the pilots I saw were not a very aggressive group, or they did not have the confidence in their aircraft that the Me 109 pilots had. In August of 1943, while escorting Martin B-26 Marauders to Naples, I saw Fw 190s do a series of Immelmanns from the deck until they were well above us; that certainly displayed performance."[26]

If Focke-Wulfs were at times less than aggressive in the Mediterranean, they were generally lethal over Europe. Republic P-47 pilot Robert S. Johnson recounts the daunting appraisals he and fellow Thunderbolt pilots received on arrival in England:

"Oh, wonderful!" he writes in *Thunderbolt!* "Just the news we needed most to hear. We argued vehemently with the British pilots; an argument which, we hoped, would result in a less dire forecast of the Thunderbolt's failure in combat. To no avail. 'Look, fellows,' [a Spitfire pilot] said. 'We're flying the Spit Mark Five. She's a beautiful fighter, and an angel on the controls. But the truth is that the Focke-Wulf 190 has been running us ragged. The 190 can outclimb us, and can dive faster. It packs a heavier wallop than the Spit; after all, the Jerry has four cannon and two heavy guns on his side. The only thing the Jerry can't do is turn inside us, but in every other respect the 190 has it all over the Five.'"[27]

In a single year, Bob Johnson became America's second leading ETO (European theater of operations) ace. He did it the hard way, flying when the Luftwaffe was at its peak, and all but four of his twenty-eight victories were German single-seaters. His most harrowing experience came on June

Captain Robert S. Johnson had a harrowing encounter with an Fw 190 on June 26, 1943. With twenty-eight confirmed victories, he became the second highest-scoring American ace in the ETO. Courtesy of USAF. (SI 86-4240; USAF 51225 AC)

26, 1943, when he participated in the 56th Fighter Group's escort coverage of a B-17 mission to Villacoublay.

Johnson saw sixteen Focke-Wulfs diving from the rear, but nobody heard his call for a break. Maintaining formation with the other unheeding Thunderbolts, he took a terrible pounding from 20-mm cannon shells; it seemed to him that an avalanche of boulders slammed into his rugged fighter, shattering the canopy and sending him tumbling out of control. The explosions continued as his pursuer followed him down, and in between cannon shots there came a continuous hail of machine gun fire.

Unable to bail out because the shredded canopy had jammed, he plunged through and somehow missed the Flying Fortress formation. He fought panic as flames swirled at his face through the shattered plexiglass. Oil smeared his windshield and hydraulic fluid from broken lines stung his swollen eyes. When the fire somehow burned itself out, he got the riddled P-47 into a controlled descent heading more or less for home. Time and again he strained against the jammed canopy and the plane heeled sickeningly off to the side, forcing him to bring it back under control. It was then that he had his unforgettable experience.

"My heart again is in my throat," he stated. "A fighter, alone. I am close to the Channel, *so* close, as I stare at the approaching machine. Slightly behind the Thunderbolt, closing in from four o'clock at about 8,000 feet, a fighter closes in. I squint my eyes, trying to make out details. The fighter slides still closer.

"Never have I seen so beautiful an airplane. A rich, dappled blue, from a dark, threatening thunderstorm to a light sky blue. The cowling is a brilliant, gleaming yellow. Beautiful, and death on the wing. A Focke-Wulf 190, one of Göring's Boys on the prowl after the raging air battle from which I have been blasted, and slicing through the air—at me. I stare at the airplane, noting the wax coating gleaming on the wings and body."[28]

It was indeed one of the elite Abbeville Boys of JG 26 that pulled up on his wing to inspect the stricken Jug. Then the German wheeled around to line up fifty yards off Johnson's tail. The American instantly hit the height adjustment to drop his seat, pulled in his arms, and braced himself for the attack. It came with a stream of bullets to his wings and fuselage, bullets that slammed against the armor plating at his back, which was all that kept him alive. It was now clear that the German was out of shells for his four 20-mm cannon, and so could only use his less-effective twin 7.9-mm (approximately .30-caliber) machine guns.

When the attack broke off, the blue Focke-Wulf again slipped alongside. Johnson rammed the rudded pedals in turn, fishtailing to kill speed, and dropped behind his adversary but couldn't see to aim; the fire of his eight 50-caliber guns went wide. He watched the German plane climb away and sweep back in like a shark to again take up station off his wingtip.

"The Focke-Wulf inches in closer," he wrote, "gleaming blue wing sitting over mine, the top so close I can almost lean out of the cockpit and touch the waxed metal. I stare across the scant feet separating our two planes. Our eyes lock, then his gaze travels over the Thunderbolt, studying the fighter from nose to tail. No need to wonder what he is thinking. He is amazed that my airplane still flies; I know his astonishment that I am in the air. Each time his gaze scans the Thunderbolt he shakes his head, mystified. For at such close range he can see the tears and holes, the blackened and scorched metal from the fire, the oily film covering the nose and the windscreen, the shattered canopy."[29]

Incredibly, the German fighter made two more unsuccessful attacks on the helpless P-47 before finally giving up and breaking off over the English Channel. Robert Johnson watched in relief, his respect for the Focke-Wulf outweighed only by the affection he held for the rugged Thunderbolt.

And what of the Mustang? This superb North American fighter was intentionally a bit less maneuverable than it might have been, because its designers opted for sufficient stability to make it viable for brutally tiring long-range escort missions. Mustangs flew to the heart of Germany and back, whereas Focke-Wulfs, Messerschmitts, and Spitfires were severely limited in combat radius by an endurance of only about ninety minutes. In contrast to these tactical and defensive fighters, the P-51 was a tremendously effective offensive strategic weapon; its phenomenal range made American daylight bombing possible and spelled an end to Germany's industrial base. That the Mustang could fly for eight hours and still mix it on even terms with the best Luftwaffe fighters is truly remarkable.

It was 11:45 a.m. on March 5, 1944. Captain William R. O'Brien was leading the 363rd Fighter Squadron's Blue Flight on B-24 escort north of Bordeaux when a mixed flight of Bf 109s and Fw 190s attacked from six o'clock high. The number four man in Blue Flight was Flight Officer Charles E. Yeager, one of the 357th Fighter Group's original pilots, who had just the day before shot down his first enemy aircraft over Berlin. Yeager called "Break, break" over the radio and O'Brien turned toward the second aircraft in the German formation.[30]

O'Bee, as the popular twenty-two-year-old pilot was known, followed the Focke-Wulf down as it split-essed. He opened fire and called his wing man for cover but could get no answer, so he continued firing before breaking straight up to avoid solid clouds ahead. Large pieces of the Fw 190 damaged his wing man's Mustang, and something big—he didn't know what—barely missed his own.

"I did a stupid thing of letting my airspeed drop down to about 150 mph before rolling out," recalls O'Brien. "When I rolled out, I looked for my wing man, Bob Moore, and found him. In back of him was a '109. I don't know how long he had been with us. Maybe it is just as well I don't. We ran

On March 5, 1944, Captain William R. "O'Bee" O'Brien shot down the Focke-Wulf that shot down Flight Officer Charles E. "Chuck" Yeager. An ace by war's end, O'Brien is shown here in the cockpit of his P-51 Mustang. Courtesy of William R. O'Brien. (SI 86-1192)

the '109 off and headed home. I could transmit but not receive radio signal and Moore was just the opposite. This is why he did not answer my call for cover. We limped into Ford Airfield (RAF) that afternoon in bad weather with sour engines."[31]

As it turned out, O'Bee downed the Focke-Wulf that moments before had shot down Chuck Yeager. Being "hacked" over enemy territory was a minor setback for Yeager, now famous as the first man to fly faster than sound; he arrived back at base two months later, ready to fly and better-fed than before. Squadron mates O'Brien and Yeager, both aces, still share a healthy respect for their erstwhile adversary.

Interestingly, a year later General Yeager found himself at Wright Field, Dayton, Ohio, assigned the delightful task of flying captured enemy aircraft. His strong opinions of the twenty-five or so Japanese and German aircraft are summed up in a single sentence: "The Focke-Wulf 190 was the only one in the same league with the Mustang."[32]

By mid-1943, captured Focke-Wulfs were already finding their way to the United States. Most went to Wright Field in Dayton, Ohio, which was home to the U.S. Army Air Forces' Flight Test Center. Like Farnborough in England and Erprobungsstelle Rechlin in Germany, Wright Field housed within its high-security gates countless accelerated wartime projects and addressed the critical wartime intelligence duty of enemy aircraft evaluation. The demands of this task were so great that Eglin Field in Florida became a secondary center of USAAF foreign aircraft evaluation.

Brigadier General Gustav "Gus" Lundquist ranks among the best of these elite Fighter Test Division test pilots. He was a major when he strapped into Fw 190G EB-104, the second of two captured examples that arrived at Wright Field on August 5, 1943.

"I made several flights in the Fw 190G in late 1943 and early 1944," he states. "Although not quite in a class with our P-51, I found the Fw 190G nevertheless to be a first-class fighter aircraft in every respect, and certainly a step up from the Me 109E and Me 109G that I also flew at Wright Field. The Fw 190G didn't have the high-altitude capability of our P-51 or P-47, but from 25,000 feet down it was a formidable combat aircraft in the hands of a competent combat pilot."[33]

Majors Gustav "Gus" Lundquist and P. A. "Fred" Borsodi were among the USAAF pilots assigned to test fly captured Focke-Wulfs at Wright Field in 1944. Behind them is EB-104, an Fw 190 G-3 with bomb racks removed. (SI 80-20359)

Gus Lundquist left for England soon after in a Spitfire Mark IX reworked at Wright Field to have sufficient range to escort American bombers to Berlin and back (this secret modification is today all but forgotten because it ruined the famous British fighter's flying characteristics). While overseas, the eager American test pilot engaged in an unauthorized fight with two Messerschmitt Bf 109s and spent the rest of the war as a POW.

Lundquist remembers the Focke-Wulf with special fondness. "I liked flying the Fw 190G. Like the P-51, it was a pilot's airplane with an excellent cockpit layout, good visibility, excellent control response, excellent maneuverability, and a wide-stance landing gear which made landing a lot less dicey than landing the Me 109 with its narrower undercarriage."[34]

Captain Kenneth Chilstrom was a twenty-two-year-old veteran of P-40 and A-36 combat operations in North Africa, Sicily, and Italy when he reported to Wright Field's Fighter Test Division in 1943. There his daily flying included Spitfires, Zeros, Corsairs; rare experimental types like the XP-55, XP-60, and XP-77; and almost every fighter the Army Air Forces flew, as well as an occasional bomber for good measure. He spent six years there, and as a major was for a period chief of the fighter division.

"All of us who flew the Fw 190 were very impressed with the handling characteristics, particularly the rate of roll," Ken Chilstrom remembers. "It was better than that of U.S. and British fighters. The Fw 190 was truly a fighter pilot's airplane; you liked the cockpit, engine operation, and unilever throttle—everything but the weak brakes. I liked the Focke-Wulf much more than the Me 109."[35]

The single-lever throttle was a unique feature. The Focke-Wulf had a hydraulic mechanical computer called the "brain box" that automatically set mixture, propeller pitch, boost, and magneto timing for maximum efficiency. Fw 190 pilots consequently had a lower workload than pilots in other air forces; there was just the throttle to worry about. The drawback was that there were constant minor surges that made the Fw 190 harder to fly in close formation.

In 1944, an Fw 190 was supplied by Wright Field's Air Technical Intelligence Division to the Bell Aircraft Company. The plane was flown to Buffalo, New York, where Bell personnel made a thorough evaluation of the airframe.

Major Kenneth Chilstrom, in the cockpit of an Fw 190 D-9, discusses flight test duties with Captain Robert Baird. Chilstrom, a veteran of P-40 and A-36 combat, shared the universally high opinion of the German fighter held by Allied pilots who flew it. Courtesy of Kenneth Chilstrom. (SI 85-11318)

Another captured example was the Fw 190 A-5 (misidentified at the time as an A-4) flown by the U.S. Navy in mock combat trials against the Vought F4U-1 Corsair and Grumman F6F-3 Hellcat fighters. If one is tempted to wonder how first-line European and Pacific theater fighter aircraft might have fared had they ever met in combat, here is one fascinating answer.

The Focke-Wulf that was the focus of this study was requested by the Technical Air Intelligence Section of Naval Intelligence. It arrived at the Captured Enemy Aircraft Unit, Naval Air Station Anacostia in Washington, D.C., on January 24, 1944. The former Luftwaffe machine was in good shape although stripped of armament, radios, and various other parts. During the next month, the CEAU made repairs to the fuselage, wings, engine, canopy, and electrical system after which—resplendent in a bright paint scheme with large American stars and a striped rudder—it was flown to the Naval Air Test Center at Patuxent River Naval Air Station on February 25, 1944.

In all probability an Fw 190 A-5/U8, this Focke-Wulf had been employed as a fighter-bomber with bomb racks (removed after capture) and without cannon armament. Using a captured German handbook as a guide, ballast was used to bring the German aircraft to the proper gross weight and balance for a standard fighter version. At Patuxent, it was repainted in the standard three-tone camouflage scheme for Navy fighters.

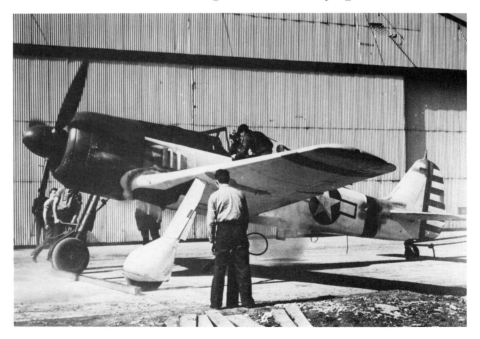

U.S. Naval personnel stand by with fire extinguishers as a brightly painted Fw 190 A-5, restored at NAS Anacostia in Washington, D.C., starts up on February 25, 1944, for a flight to the Naval Air Test Center at NAS Patuxent River. Courtesy of National Archives. (SI 86-3840)

The same aircraft flies southeast en route to NAS Patuxent River in southern Maryland. The nose appears to be red, while the rudder features the standard prewar American pattern of alternating red and white horizontal bands and a vertical blue stripe. (SI 86-6291)

Project pilots Lieutenant Commander F. L. Palmer and Lieutenants C. C. Andrews and W. C. Holmes flew a rigorous series of tests that revealed that the Focke-Wulf easily outclimbed the two Navy fighters. Moreover, while the German fighter and the Hellcat had an identical top speed of 334 mph on the deck, the Fw 190 became progressively faster at altitude until, at 25,000 feet, it attained 410 mph compared to the F6F's 391 mph. The Corsair fared better at low altitude, being 29 mph faster on the deck, but was still somewhat slower at 25,000 feet with a top speed of 403 mph.

In rate of roll, the Corsair (with the help of its mechanically boosted ailerons) and the Fw 190 were about even, whereas the F6F was slower.

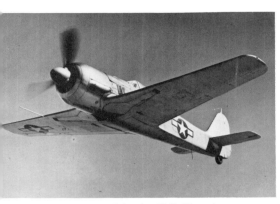

Repainted in the U.S. Navy's standard three-tone paint scheme, this Focke-Wulf flew extensively at "Pax River" (the Naval equivalent of Wright Field). In comparative flight trials at 25,000 feet (the Focke-Wulf's best altitude) the German fighter reached 410 mph, bettering the Navy's F4U Corsair and F6F Hellcat fighters which attained 403 mph and 391 mph respectively. (SI 86-594)

Both Navy fighters, however, had far superior turning characteristics; there was no maneuver the Fw 190 could do that they couldn't easily follow, whereas the German plane stalled out trying to keep on the tails of the American fighters.

In a sharp slow turn to the left, the Focke-Wulf was subject to aileron reversal and a sudden stall. In a similar turn to the right, it tended to drop the right wing and nose, and enter a dive. If stalls were sudden, however, recovery was simple.

The cockpit was deemed cramped by American standards, although functional and very well laid out. Perhaps the best feature in this regard was the pilot's low seat, which left the pilot sitting with his legs forward and high, a position that minimized the effects of blackout. Vision was considered adequate but limited because the Fw 190's low windscreen extended only some six inches above the cowling contour; forward vision from the other two types—even the "hose-nose" Corsair—was found to be superior. Although rearward visibility in the German fighter was the best of the three, the absence of a rear-view mirror was lamented. As the Revi gunsight was missing from this A-5, sighting could not be evaluated, although all pilots agreed that it would be an excellent gun platform.

Significantly, it was observed that formation flying was extremely difficult because the single power lever deprived the pilot of fine engine control. Other conclusions in the final report, dated April 1944, are as follows:

> The general opinion of the pilots who made the comparative tests is that the Fw 190 is an extremely simple airplane to fly and it is designed for pilot convenience, but is not equal to the F4U-1 or F6F-3 in combat. The simplicity of the cockpit in the Fw 190 was in contrast to the cockpits of the F4U-1 and F6F-3. However, it is felt that although more automatic features are provided in the Fw 190, less direct control over variable settings is provided and the pilot has, as a result, less actual control over the engine performance. All the pilots agree that the F4U-1 and F6F-3 would be preferred in actual combat operations.
>
> In view of the fact that the Fw 190 can outrun the F4U-1 and F6F-3 in a 160 knot, or faster climb, the best solution in offense is for the F4U-1 and F6F-3 to get the Fw 190 to close with them so that advantage can be taken of their superior maneuverability, provided, of course, that any initial advantage in altitude is not sacrificed merely for the sake of closing. When being attacked from astern, the Fw 190 can be expected to roll and dive out from attack.

Another view of the U.S. Navy's Fw 190 A-5 shows that the German fighter's pleasing lines are, if anything, enhanced by its "Hellcat" paint job. (SI 86-595)

Lieutenant Arthur G. Johnson, 52nd Fighter Group, stands before the P-51B in which he became an ace in the MTO (Mediterranean theater of operations). Johnson shot down two Fw 190s while escorting B-17s and B-24s from Foggia, Italy, to Ploesti, Romania, on May 31, 1944. Courtesy of Arthur G. Johnson. (SI 85-11317)

If attacked by the Fw 190, the F4U-1 and F6F-3 can evade by the use of tight turns. When followed by the Fw 190 the F4U and F6F can evade by the use of tight loops. If the Fw 190 attempts to follow the other airplanes in tight loops it stalls out.

In general, whenever the hit-and-run technique cannot be employed, the F4U and F6F should make every effort to close with the Fw 190, in both offense and defense.[36]

Captain Arthur G. Johnson was a flight leader in the 52nd Fighter Group's 2nd Fighter Squadron, which operated from Madna near Foggia, Italy. On the last day of May 1944, he was headed northeast over the Adriatic Sea in his P-51B, escorting Fifteenth Air Force B-17s and B-24s on a mission to bomb German oil refineries at Ploesti, Romania.

It was over Ploesti that he sighted two Focke-Wulfs flying approximately fifty feet apart. Johnson broke formation to engage them from the rear but the fighters, obviously flown by experienced Luftwaffe pilots, chopped their throttles and dumped their flaps. Johnson missed a chance to shoot; his initial reaction, to slow down also, instantly gave way to his throwing the throttle wide open and executing a loop to avoid their fire.

"Also at the instant that I passed," he writes, "I noticed the bright yellow paint covering their engine nacelles, and the brief thought went through my mind that these might be Göring's elite 'Abbeville Boys' that we had heard so much about. These recollections are vivid because of the shrewdness and skill in their maneuver and the horrible thought that my luck had just run out."[37]

At full power in the top of the loop, he looked and saw the Fw 190s pulling condensation streamers from their wing tips in their haste to catch up. They shot but didn't have the necessary deflection, and as he came down the backside of the loop they were diving for the deck in an apparent attempt to run for home.

"At the moment that my loop maneuver brought me once more around on their tail," he states, "my reaction changed from 'get the hell out of here' to pursuit in order to engage them in a dogfight. I was now on their tails ever closer to the ground; I fired at them, disintegrating the first one. At this point, I was within 800 to 1,000 feet of the ground and the whole incident had probably taken twenty seconds. I began to climb out and turn toward Italy."[38]

When he got back to base after almost six hours of flying, his wing man confirmed that the second Focke-Wulf had also crashed as a result of the attack. Johnson finished the war an ace, and went on to became a doctor. There is no doubt in his mind that he had the superior aircraft.

Captain John J. Voll, the highest-scoring Fifteenth Air Force ace, downed no less than twenty-one enemy aircraft in just fifty-seven missions with the 31st Fighter Group between May and December 1944. Among this twenty-two-year-old pilot's victories were nine Focke-Wulfs. He knew from personal experience that the Fw 190 would pull away from his P-51 *American Beauty* in a dive, but the Mustang always caught up at the bottom. The Mustang could also stay with the Focke-Wulf even in the most violent maneuvering. The only other Axis fighter he considered nearly as good was the Italian Macchi 202 or 205.

"The Fw 190 was the best fighter the Germans had," he asserts emphatically. "It was much better than the Me 109."[39]

Finally, there is George "Max" Lamb, who on March 23, 1945, led two flights of 354th Fighter Group P-51s covering Allied forces crossing a pontoon bridge over the Rhine River south of Metz, France. Despite broken

60

Focke-Wulf Fw 190Ds were captured and flown by Soviet pilots in World War II. These machines, photographed at Marienburg, Germany, in the spring of 1945, probably belonged to the combat squadron of captured aircraft reported to have operated on the Black Sea. Courtesy of Carl-Fredrik Geust. (SI 86-3808)

cloud layers, he saw enemy aircraft high up and to his right. They were Fw 190Ds, the "Doras" they had heard so much about. Lamb sent one of his flights after the high group while he engaged the lower with his remaining three aircraft.

In the wild dogfighting that followed, Lamb let his wing man destroy one, and then he himself shot down three more. Much of the tail unit of one plane he destroyed somehow passed through his propeller to bounce off his bullet-proof canopy, but he was not hurt. In all, his flight claimed nine enemy aircraft with no loss to their own ranks, completely routing German aerial opposition to the bridge.

Lamb, awarded a medal for superior airmanship and brilliant leadership,[40] saw even this advanced version of the Focke-Wulf as no serious competition for his Mustangs. He remembers them instead for quite another reason.

"They were, in fact, the aircraft I most admired," he recalls. "The Fw 190 was a beautiful airplane!"[41]

A Soviet officer stands before a Focke-Wulf Fw 190 F-8/R1; other captured Fw 190Ds and Fs recede into the distance. The immediate postwar years saw continued Soviet use of captured Focke-Wulfs, especially Ta 152s, which addressed a Soviet need for a high-altitude interceptor. (SI 86-3807)

This Fw 190 F-9, wearing markings indicating it to have belonged to a group technical officer, is run up by a 356th Fighter Group pilot at Munich, late May 1945. Like many captured machines, this one ended up a group "hack" that amused American pilots waiting to be rotated home. Courtesy of Hess Bomberger. (SI 86-3802)

4

The Immediate Postwar Era

The war in Europe ended on May 8, 1945. With the cessation of hostilities, the U.S. Army Air Forces initiated a unique project called "Operation Lusty" under the able command of Colonel Harold E. Watson. Hal Watson was a superb pilot with engineering experience who possessed the dashing good looks of a Hollywood lead (he was actually screen tested before the war, but flying held more fascination for him than acting). His enviable job was to round up captured German aircraft for return to the United States.

Watson gathered together a team of hot pilots that became known as "Watson's Whizzers." Among the flying machines they recovered from every corner of the European continent was the National Air and Space Museum's Fw 190 F-8. No records exist to state where it might have been

Perhaps the most colorful Focke-Wulf in North Africa, this Fw 190 A-5 Trop was the prized possession of 85th Fighter Squadron, 79th Fighter Group, pilots who undoubtedly found it substantially faster and more maneuverable than their Curtiss P-40s. This aircraft has a red nose ring, spinner, and wing and stabilizer tips. Its rudder has red, white, and blue stripes. (SI A 43,569-G)

Colonel (later Major General) Harold E. "Hal" Watson, the AAF pilot responsible for rounding up German aircraft at war's end, leans with his hand on the horizontal stabilizer of a derelict Fw 190 F-8, W.-Nr. 930 860. Beside him is Brigadier (later four-star) General Mark E. Bradley. (SI 85-9477)

Luftwaffe aircraft remaining at the cessation of hostilities did not last long. Here, a Focke-Wulf that bellied into a Czechoslovakian field awaits the scrapper's torch. Courtesy of Peter Petrick. (SI 86-3828)

In the aftermath of war, a couple inspects a crashed Fw 190 F-8 in Yugoslavia. The desire to forget soon led to the scrapping of German aircraft throughout the once-great extent of the Third Reich. Courtesy of Heinz J. Nowarra. (SI 86-3826)

Late in the war, Fw 190s were mounted atop Junkers Ju 88s loaded with high explosives. Called Mistel, the resulting composite aircraft was intended to counter American bomber formations; after setting the Ju 88 on course into a formation, where it would detonate, the Fw 190 would pull away and return for a normal landing. Courtesy of USAF. (SI 86-3836; USAF 58019 AC)

picked up; in all probability, it was flown to Germany proper from its last operational base somewhere along the nearby collapsing eastern front. In any event, it joined a large assemblage of other planes being hoisted onto the deck of the British aircraft carrier HMS *Reaper* at Cherbourg, France, for delivery to Newark, New Jersey. Arriving in late July 1945, this anonymous Fw 190 was transported by ground to Freeman Field in Seymour, Indiana.

Freeman Army Air Field is all but forgotten today, but in the immediate postwar years it was a beehive of fascinating activity. German, Japanese, British, and Italian aircraft filled its hangars or graced its runways, their unusual engines bellowing. It all began when Chief of the U.S. Army Air Forces Henry H. "Hap" Arnold decreed early in 1945 that foreign aircraft and equipment be preserved within the United States. Wright Field's Air Technical Service Command, which had been responsible for foreign equipment evaluation since 1941, was the agency entrusted with the ambitious goal of obtaining, as stated by Major General Oliver Echols, *"at least one (1) each of every type of item used by the Enemy Air Forces* [original italics]."[1]

All existing hangars at Wright Field and nearby Clinton County Army Air Field were already in use, and the ATSC's single hangar at Dayton Army Air Field at Vandalia was hopelessly inadequate; much of the foreign equipment collection, including at that time sixteen active and eleven inactive airplanes, was stored outdoors in odd corners of all three bases.[2] With huge new infusions of foreign aircraft and equipment expected,[3] drastic measures were necessary. Consequently, the disused Freeman Field was reactivated on June 16, 1945, under the command of Colonel H. C. Dorney. As preparing and maintaining aircraft in flyable condition for evaluation at Wright and Eglin Fields was to be a key function, full maintenance and machine shop facilities were provided. German and Japanese airplanes used metric threads and standards, so having the capability to manufacture missing parts was essential.

A few of Wright Field's foreign aircraft sit in the sun in 1945. Appearing from left to right are a Mitsubishi A6M-3 Hamp, Focke-Wulf Fw 190A, Hawker Typhoon, Messerschmitt Me 410A, and Junkers Ju 88D. Courtesy of Ken Chilstrom. (SI 85-13049)

Arriving in Dayton, Ohio, on August 5, 1943, Fw 190A EB-101 was the first Focke-Wulf to fly at Wright Field, the U.S. Army Air Forces' Flight Test Center. Courtesy of Ken Chilstrom. (SI 85-13048)

EB-101 streaks over its new home at Wright Field. This aircraft was a darling of Fighter Section test pilots, many of whom were fighter aces who had completed their operational tours of duty. (SI 86-6288)

64

This extremely rare photograph illustrates the best American and German single-engine fighters together in one flight. From top to bottom, they are the North American P-51D Mustang, Messerschmitt Bf 109F, Republic P-47D Thunderbolt, and Focke-Wulf Fw 190A. (SI 86-6287)

Although it arrived on the same day as EB-101, Fw 190 G-3 EB-104 (DN+FP, W.-Nr. 160 016) was not restored to flightworthy condition until January 12, 1944. This aircraft, a Jabo-Rei, was stripped of its bomb racks. It is shown on the Fighter Branch's Flight Section ramp minutes before its first flight. (SI 86-3832)

Wright Field's Fw 190 G-3 soon became a favorite mount of American pilots. Fighter Section test pilots included Richard Bong, Francis Gabreski, Don Gentile, Chuck Yeager, and Bob Hoover. (SI 77-49)

Lieutenant Colonel Barney Estes, chief of Wright Field's Fighter Branch, climbs into Fw 190 G-3 EB-104 for a test flight. (SI 86-3825)

Any pilot who wears sunglasses and a baseball cap just has to be an American. This photograph shows EB-104 in flight over Ohio farmland, early in 1944. (SI A 48623-C)

Seen from below, EB-104 G-3 clearly shows where its wing bomb racks were removed. As was often done with captured machines, and at times by the Germans themselves, this aircraft is being flown without the panel that covers the wheel well between the tires. Courtesy of USAF. (SI 86-3829; USAF D-26721 AC)

The ATSC's Fighter Test Division soon had altogether a dozen Fw 190s: The two Focke-Wulfs returned to the United States before the cessation of hostilities in Europe—Fw 190A EB-101 and Fw 190 G-3 EB-104, which arrived on August 5, 1943—had been thoroughly wrung out by Wright Field test pilots in comparative flights against American aircraft types. By September 1945, ten more Fw 190s, coded FE-112 through FE-121,[4] were there. The Fw 190F later to be restored by the National Air and Space Museum was coded FE-117.

At any one time there were some eighty-five to ninety different aircraft on the ramp, twenty or so foreign. Among the pilots with the enviable duty of flying these planes at one time or another were Gus Lundquist and Ken Chilstrom (see chapter 3). There were also aces Richard Bong, Francis Gabreski, Don Gentile, Chuck Yeager, and John Godfrey. And there was the now-famous airshow pilot and aerobatic champion Bob Hoover, who was denied his chance to be an ace by a stay in a German POW camp. On the more senior side there were Colonels Al Boyd and Ben Kelsey, perhaps the two most experienced American test pilots of all.

With the end of World War II in the summer of 1945, test flying of captured aircraft suddenly had a much lower priority; the desire to forget

Fw 190 D-9 FE-121 was also restored to flightworthy condition at Wright Field. This aircraft, which no longer survives, is shown being run up before a crowd of onlookers. Courtesy of National Archives. (SI 86-3788)

Perhaps the rarest Focke-Wulf still in existence is Ta 152H FE-112. This machine remains disassembled and in storage at the Paul E. Garber Facility in Maryland, awaiting restoration by the National Air and Space Museum. Courtesy of National Archives. (SI 86-3833)

the war was universal, and consequently many flyable aircraft were not used. FE-117 was just such a machine; remanufactured with Freeman Field's vast stock of replacement parts by experienced mechanics to like-new condition, it was placed directly into storage.

Out of the dozen Focke-Wulfs at Wright and Freeman Fields (only two of which flew extensively), a full quarter survive in the collection of the National Air and Space Museum. In addition to FE-117, there are Ta 152H FE-112 (awaiting restoration at the Garber Facility) and Fw 190 D-9 FE-120 (currently on loan to the Air Force Museum at Wright-Patterson Air Force Base, in Dayton, Ohio).[5]

Sporting a fictitious camouflage and missing its spinner, Fw 190 F-8 FE-116 sits on the ramp at Wright Field. The open cowling suggests that maintenance was being performed. No photographs of FE-117, the NASM F-8, at Wright Field are known to exist. Courtesy of David Meyer. (SI 86-3801)

5

Restoration

In August 1980, the hottest part of a muggy Washington summer, thirty-five years of storage ended for Fw 190 F-8 FE-117, the National Air and Space Museum's ground attack Focke-Wulf. The disassembled airplane was brought into Building 10, the triple-bay restoration shop of the Museum's Paul E. Garber Facility in Silver Hill, Maryland.

The first order of business was to confirm if it was indeed, as believed, an F-8 model. The FuG 16ZY radio equipment, bulged canopy, wing racks, and absence of outboard wing cannon supported the supposition. A look inside turned up other strong evidence; F-8s had A-7 fuselages until March 1944, when they incorporated improved A-8 fuselages, in which a third internal fuel tank became standard. The NASM airplane had a third tank.

Eight miles away on the Mall in Washington, D.C., curators at the National Air and Space Museum began an extremely difficult research project. Frustrating the effort was the fact that, at the end of the European war, the German High Command had issued general orders that all papers were to be destroyed. With the execution of these orders, unit histories, production figures, and countless other records were forever lost to posterity.

Among the most frustrating losses were record cards maintained on aircraft in the Luftwaffe inventory. Had they survived, these cards would have provided the entire history of Fw 190 F-8 FE-117; among the information one might have extracted from them is when and where the NASM machine was produced, to what units it had been assigned, who flew it on what operational missions, what damage was sustained, where repairs were effected, and so on.

The painstaking research process did eventually tell curators that their Fw 190F Werk-Nummer 931 884 began life as Fw 190A W.-Nr. 640 069, more specifically as an A-5 through A-8 model with the A-7 series being

This photograph taken in the 1960s shows the fuselage of FE-117 already in a somewhat deteriorated condition. (SI A 2175-B)

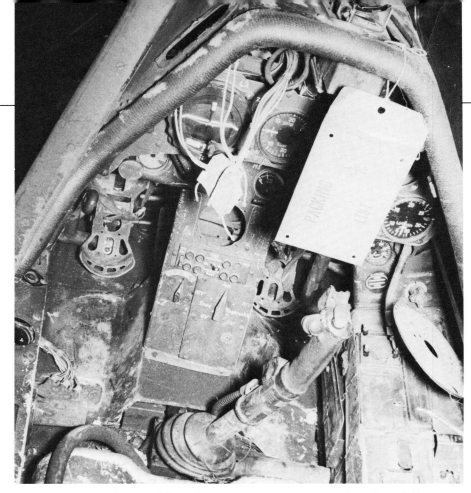

A view of the cockpit from the same period shows the plane to be essentially complete. The German radios and oxygen equipment attest to the fact that this plane was never flown at Wright or Freeman Fields, where the standard practice was to replace these systems with their more reliable and easily serviced American counterparts. (SI A 2175-19A)

A plate found inside the fuselage of the NASM Fw 190 clearly shows the earlier Werk-Nummer to have been 640 069. Reconstructions of wartime serial number blocks suggest that the NASM machine may have been an Fw 190 A-7 before it was rebuilt as an F-8. (SI 82-3-10)

likely (see appendix 6), although some sources suggest that few A-7s were produced. In any event, Fw 190 A-4 and earlier models could certainly be ruled out, as they were structurally shorter, had smaller rear fuselage access doors, and had an earlier type of RLM serial number.

Its markings suggest that Fw 190A W.-Nr. 640 069 entered service as a staff aircraft with the zweite Gruppe of an operational Jagdgeschwader in 1943. Its desert tan camouflage further suggests that it served in the Mediterranean theater or the Balkans. At some point, this Focke-Wulf apparently suffered such severe damage to the wings that it was written off and rebuilt as an entirely new machine. Such recycling—standard practice in the German aircraft industry—continues to plague aviation historians anxious to accurately comprehend Germany's wartime industrial prowess. Recycling was certainly a logical expedient since, in contrast to Allied losses, downed Luftwaffe aircraft generally fell back on their own soil where they could be recovered.

Arado at Warnemünde (one of many plants producing Fw 190s under license) probably performed the remanufacture. As the machine just before it on the production line, W.-Nr. 931 883, is known to have carried the factory codes KT+ZR, FE-117 was at that time probably officially listed as KT+ZS, although these markings were probably not applied to the airframe; wartime expediency dictated that the machine retain its earlier paint scheme during remanufacture.

No longer an interceptor but rather a ground attack machine, Fw 190 F-8/R1, W.-Nr. 931 884 rolled out of the factory—for the second time in its checkered career—in early 1944. Special modifications for its role included fuselage and wing bomb racks and almost eight hundred pounds of additional armor to protect it, primarily from fire from below. Some time after its completion, this machine was painted in the unusual and attractive color scheme that it today wears again (see the restoration section of this chapter).

As indicated by the yellow V under the left wing, 931 884 was almost

A photograph of a captured Fw 190 plant hints at the past of NASM's F-8. Machines wearing operational markings share the assembly line with new airframes, confirming the German practice of salvaging airframes downed in combat and rebuilding them as "new" aircraft. Courtesy of USAF. (SI 86-3824; USAF 91416 AC)

Fw 190 F-8 W.-Nr. 931 883, one digit less than the NASM F-8, serves as a photographic prop for a member of the Royal Air Force in Schleswig-Holstein, September 1945. Courtesy of Air Britain via Thomas H. Hitchcock. (SI 85-18837)

certainly assigned to Schlachtgeschwader 2 on the eastern front, most probably joining this wing's erste Gruppe, commanded by Knight's Cross holder Major Heinz Frank, in the spring of 1944. Further supporting this supposition is the fact that Werk-Nummern 931 880 and 931 894 (Fw 190 F-8s from the same production block) are known to have been in service with the I./SG 2 as early as March of that year.

Of all units, it is fitting that NASM's Focke-Wulf flew with I./SG 2. This erste Gruppe was perhaps the most influential of all; it gave rise to both Generalen der Schlachtflieger, Oberstleutnant Dr. Ernst Kupfer and Oberst Hubertus Hitschhold (who left it in mid-1942 to take over command of SG 1). The wing itself was the oldest and most experienced ground attack unit in the Luftwaffe, dating back to the Fliegertruppe Schwerin of 1934. In various structurings, it served in Spain, Poland, France, the Battle of Britain, the Mediterranean (zweite Gruppe only), the U.S.S.R., and Eastern Europe. Schlachtgeschwader 2 was primarily engaged in the southern sector of the Russian front, the scene of the fiercest Soviet aerial opposition; it was here that Kozhedub and Pokryshkin flew, for example. There can be little doubt that the Immelmann wing did a heavy share of the fighting in the east. During FE-117's tenure with the unit later in the war, SG 2 was commanded by the most successful ground attack pilot of all time, Oberst Hans Ulrich Rudel.

At the outset of the actual restoration, veteran craftsmen Joe Fichera, Mike Lyons, and Dale Bucy surveyed the sorry machine with mixed feelings. The prospect of three years of arduous labor was daunting, but buoying their spirits was the excitement that always accompanies such rare and demanding challenges.

Joe Fichera, the team leader, is a legend. Among "antiquers" or vintage airplane enthusiasts, he is revered for his knowledge, his unexcelled personal restorations, and the hangars of rare flying machines he is reputed to have. Two wings, open cockpits, and chuttering radial engines put a blissful smile on his face. Fichera's voice is soft and measured, his word law. He can tell you what engine any ancient ingition harness or exhaust manifold came from, how to properly rig a Curtiss Jenny, or what end of an earth inductor compass points up; this knowledge extends unfailingly to warplanes although he loves the gentler machines far more.

The late Mike Lyons, like Joe Fichera, was very familiar with German World War II airplanes; he had not long before worked on the restoration of the Museum's rare Messerschmitt Me 262 jet fighter. Quiet, fun, and immensely likeable, he never had fewer than two new jokes to tell. The skill and patience he displayed as a craftsman also served him well in the construction of prize-winning models, where his love of aviation found beautiful expression. Already ill at the time of the restoration, Mike died of cancer in November 1984.

The team's youngest member, Dale Bucy, is proof that the guild system is alive and well. Like the majority of the restorers, many of whom would also be called upon as their particular skills were needed for the Fw 190, he is continually learning more by doing, preserving the knowledge and techniques of bygone eras in aviation. His credentials were already strong, for like Mike Lyons he had worked on the Me 262.

Immediately apparent at the outset was that this machine, captured after the need for evaluation had been met by other Allied Focke-Wulfs, had not been flown. Attesting to this belief were the absence of English-language captions and American radios or oxygen equipment (it was standard practice always to replace these German components with their more-reliable and serviceable U.S. equivalents). This was a lucky break, for with the original German units still in place, the task of rounding up needed parts for the restoration would be much easier.

Work began (as it had with the Me 262) with several months of careful sanding to strip through American paint and document the successive layers of German colors beneath. However laborious, this phase was crucial because it offered Museum curators the only hope they had of learning the wartime history of their Focke-Wulf.

"I didn't sand off every bit of paint," Lyons stated. "Instead I concentrated in particular on those areas where we might expect to find something."[1]

Perhaps the most innovative technique used to locate markings was that suggested and employed by Dale Hrabak, the Museum's chief photographer. Using infra-red film, Hrabak found traces that helped Mike Lyons zero in on, among other things, the original Werk-Nummer on the vertical stabilizer.

Infrared photography is one interesting technique used to locate and document markings covered by successive layers of paint. When sanding revealed traces of a Werk-Nummer, NASM's Chief Photographer Dale Hrabak revealed an image hidden to human eyes. (SI 80-15151-5)

After months of careful sanding to document original German paint schemes, the airframe was stripped entirely so that restoration could begin. Wearing safety gear, Joe Fichera strips a wing of the Focke-Wulf. (SI 81-6493-5A)

The picture that emerged was a fascinating one: There were in all four paint schemes. The earliest, and last to be uncovered, was a warm tan with gray-green undersurfaces. There were two horizontal bars on either side of the fuselage's early-style national insignia, the forward bar pointed. The second scheme saw these bars painted out, the addition of both a yellow fuselage band and a white 7.

It was at this point, probably the spring of 1944, that the remanufacturing was performed, as evidenced by the lack of paint on the replacement wings. The basic color of the plane in its new fighter-bomber role became an unusual combination of colors Gray-Violet 75 and Black-Green 70 in a fairly standard pattern on the wings and upper fuselage. Crosses were the later wartime style consisting of outlines only, black on the fuselage and white on the wings. The number 7 and the yellow band were reapplied, though not quite matching the earlier set. Presumably in the field late in 1944, a yellow V was painted beneath the left wing, the ends of which wrapped around the leading edge to the wing's top side. Finally, during the winter of 1944-45, irregular white blotches of snow camouflage were applied to all upper surfaces.

The final paint scheme was applied in early 1945. Either because the machine was assigned to another unit, or because the snow camouflage now rendered it too visible in the spring, all upper surfaces were sprayed color Gray-Green 74. Where the bottoms of the yellow fuselage band, white 7, and yellow V still showed, a light blue was used to cover them. At this juncture the machine became known as *gelbe Zehn* with the addition of a yellow 10. It

72

appears likely that the rudder was yellow, and there may have been a white cowl stripe.

This engine cowl provided a bit more information in the detective work. Except for a yellow stripe, it was unpainted beneath the American paint. The explanation might be the German expedient of changing an engine by replacing everything forward of the engine mount as an integral unit—accessories, radiator, cowling, and all. Called *Kraft-Eier* (literally, "power eggs"), these replacement front ends made quick engine changes possible on unimproved forward airfields lacking proper facilities (see appendix 7). If such a change was indeed performed on the NASM Fw 190F, it is quite possible that the original unit—housing a new or reworked engine—flew on another airplane before the end of the war. If so, it must have been quite a colorfully mismatched machine.

Senior Curator Robert C. Mikesh (who prepares the guidelines for every restoration) selected the middle series of colors, without snow camouflage, as the post-restoration paint scheme. This Focke-Wulf Fw 190 probably spent the longest portion of its operational career wearing them, and they certainly were more attractive than the crude patchwork scheme that followed. The earlier schemes were ruled out because they were both inappropriate for an F model and incompletely documented.

Documentation of all colors and markings was ensured photographically and with tracings. Once this phase of the project was finished, the remainder of the paint was stripped and progressive disassembly began. Now came the time to determine the extent of damage and corrosion and to lay out the parameters of the job.

It was immediately evident that Dale Bucy, a first-class sheet metal worker, would have a lot to do. The damage an airplane accumulates even when not in use, commonly referred to as "hangar rash," was particularly severe because a wooden stand supporting the fuselage had collapsed after years of rotting.

"It looked like they had taken off a lot of the parts and tossed them under the fuselage," Bucy states. "When the fuselage dropped, it got nearly all the panels and cowling sections."[2]

Mike Lyons and Joe Fichera remove a self-sealing fuel tank from the Fw 190 fuselage. (SI 81-16709-7A)

Dale Bucy works to restore a fuselage panel. Extensive use of stampings in German wartime manufacture required the use of some thirty-five forming dies to repair and replicate damaged sheet metal parts. (SI 82-5780-38A)

Skilled metal worker Dale Bucy displays an original Fw 190 horizontal stabilizer (below) and the exact duplicate he fabricated (above). The F-8's stabilizer had been lent to the Air Force Museum in Ohio for use on the NASM Fw 190 D-9, also on loan there. When the original was required for the restoration, it fell to Dale to make a new unit for the Dora. (SI 82-1344-17)

Luckily, there was an extra Focke-Wulf cowling in the NASM collection. Since it was from an A-series airplane, it required some slight modification before it would be ready to install, although it was essentially correct. This unit, along with much of the rest of the airplane, went to the chemical corrosion vats for treatment by Will Powell and Bayne Rector.

It is not commonly realized that late-war copper shortages caused many Fw 190s to be skinned with a zinc-aluminum alloy rather than the universal copper-aluminum Alclad-type sheeting. As the zinc alloy would have different long-term corrosion characteristics, FE-117 was tested to see whether it warranted special treatment. Tests revealed that no such precautions were necessary, however, as in all samples copper was the bonding agent.

The under-fuselage ETC 501 bomb rack was missing from FE-117, but the support lugs and fairing holes indicated where it had been. A photograph of the airplane after its arrival in the United States clearly showed that the rack had been installed, along with an ER 4 supplemental rack that allowed four SC 50 bombs to be carried in place of a single larger bomb.

By the early 1950s, the Focke-Wulf and some sixty other World War II aircraft had joined the Smithsonian Institution's historic National Aeronautical Collection, and were being stored in a disused Douglas Aircraft Company C-54 plant at Orchard Air Force Base (today O'Hare International Airport). These planes had to be hurriedly relocated when the Korean War geared up and the factory was needed by Fairchild for C-119 production. In the haste of the move, the rack was lost.

"The bomb rack covered the juncture of wing and fuselage," Mike Lyons speculated, "and had to be removed before the plane could be disassembled for shipment. It is probably buried somewhere under O'Hare."[3]

Other missing parts included the horizontal tail surfaces, canopy, canopy rails and crank, ammunition counters, clock, and supercharger pressure gauge. The first two items had been borrowed many years before by the Air Force Museum for use on NASM's Fw 190D, which was restored and displayed. Typical of the high degree of cooperation between the Air Force and the Smithsonian, a course of action was agreed upon that worked to the mutual advantage of both museums. The horizontal stabilizer and elevators were sent immediately to NASM, where Dale Bucy fabricated exact copies from scratch, retaining the originals (which belonged to the F-8) and sending the new units back to Dayton.

"We really got lucky on the stabilizer," Dale Bucy observed. "We had to get six supporting bearings for the elevators, and going through the catalog we found out that FAG, the company that made bearings for the Luftwaffe during World War II, was still in business. We bought the very same self-aligning double-row bearing—right down to the part number—in production still."[4]

Master craftsman Mike Lyons works on the BMW 801D radial engine. Disassembly of this power plant revealed it to be very new, indicating that the NASM F-8 had experienced an engine change shortly before capture. (SI 81-366-25)

Mike Lyons works under the instrument panel mount. A light source, clipboard with notes, and a mirror faciliate work in inaccessible areas. (SI 83-570-37A)

Air Force Museum craftsmen, meanwhile, contracted to have fabricated a duplicate of the canopy on their Fw 190 D-9. This Dora (on loan from the National Air and Space Museum) had been missing a canopy when it was restored years ago, and had been completed with the unit borrowed from the then-unrestored Fw 190 F-8. Now that the F-8's turn had come for rebuilding, the Air Force Museum returned the original unit and retained the new reproduction canopy for the Dora.

The original canopy had two long cracks in it that might have sent anybody else to commercial plexiglass companies for bids to fabricate a replacement, but NASM specialist Reid Ferguson took it all in stride, calmly working his magic to make the original canopy look as good as new. He sanded the cracks to a 90-degree bevel, then poured in the commercial product PS-30 and buffed out the filled section. It is all but impossible to see evidence of the cracks. Unfortunately, however, the windshield side panels of armored glass were too far deteriorated for restoration and did have to be replaced.

As always, original components were retained wherever possible. If a part had to be replaced, it was marked "REPLACEMENT PART BY NASM" and dated, so as not to mislead future researchers.

When Dale Bucy and Mike Lyons tore down the BMW 801D radial engine, they found that it was indeed a new unit, which supported the engine-change theory. The exact subseries and serial number of the power plant could not be ascertained, however, as its manufacturer's data plate was missing. Such items are frequently taken by souvenir hunters.

"It looked internally as if the engine only had about twenty-five or thirty hours; the machining grooves on the rings weren't even worn off, and there weren't any carbon deposits on the pistons and cylinder heads," Joe Fichera stated, then smiled. "Dale did most of the metal work and Mike a lot of the detail work. I did the heavier stuff, the stuff that doesn't take any finesse. I'm a hammer and chisel type."[5]

The day-to-day progress of the restoration showed very little change over time to people touring the Garber Facility. Restoration is an agonizingly slow process in which every part is broken into its smallest components. They are then cleaned, treated against corrosion, and reassembled before being reinstalled. Every rod, wire, bolt, and plug receives the same careful attention. This work is never cosmetic; it costs far more in time and money than would be necessary to make the machine look new (as some museums do) but is necessary to fulfill the Smithsonian Institution's mission of preserving examples of past crafts and technologies for future generations.

Will Powell and Bayne Rector are pioneering corrosion control specialists whose seemingly miraculous processes are studied by other air museums around the world. They handled the cleaning and treatment of metal parts, while master machinist Harvey Napier worked nearby turning out all manner of exquisite replacement parts. One of these was the new canopy crank, copied from that of the Focke-Wulf Ta 152H that is in storage a few buildings down the line.

Sheet metal work included repairing wing leading edges, canopy frame sheeting, and hinged access panels on the new cowl. The lower forward fuselage (damaged by the fall mentioned above) also required extensive work. A large part of this task was a steel box structure inside the front center of the wheel well bay. It looked like a crumpled sheet of paper, but Bucy and metalsmith Bill Stephenson (a superb welder) carefully brought it back to its original form.

Dale Bucy also fabricated a new fuel filler cap cover, new ammunition compartment door, new wing fillets (difficult because of their compound-curve form), new antenna cap, and new fairings for two of the four ETC 50 wing bomb racks (the new fairings on the left wing fit far better than the original units reinstalled on the right wing, a disparity Bucy attributes to wartime shortages of skilled labor.

Wherever new aluminum was incorporated into the airframe, Bucy used rubber stamps created by Garber Facility personnel to replicate the original German production codes. These markings are not visible in the completed restoration, and are indicative of the extent of the Museum's efforts to ensure maximum authenticity.

"Pretty much a Detroit-style production method was used on the Focke-Wulf," Dale Bucy observed. "Whereas the Americans and Japanese used a minimum number of dies and tended to build assemblies up from flat sheet, the Germans did an extensive amount of stamping. I only had to make up four forming dies for the restoration of the Nakajima J1N1-S Irving, whereas the Fw 190 required about thirty-five."[6]

Typically, later F-8 model Focke-Wulfs had three fuel tanks. These stiff rubberized self-sealing cells were removed from the fuselage for cleaning and treatment, the first step being the removal of damaged sections. Bucy carefully beat these portions out to their original shapes before replacing them. Devcon Flexane, a commercially available form of uncured rubber, was then applied to reattach them and build back original contours. Machinist Harvey Napier made a mold of a badly deteriorated filler neck, and injection-molded a new one using a hand pump of his own fabrication; his third attempt produced a beautiful replacement part.

The Luftwaffe used three color-coded grades of aviation gasoline during the war: A 3 (light blue) was rated at 80 octane, B 4 (dark blue) was 87 octane, and C 3 (dark green) was 100 octane. Most Messerschmitt Bf 109s used B 4, but the radial-engined Fw 190s required the scarcer C 3. Most of the avgas used by Luftwaffe aircraft was made from coal and smelled awful.

"We found about ten gallons of fuel still in the airplane," Mike Lyons remembered. "We saved a gallon. It's the synthetic type that doesn't really

A legend even among master aircraft restorers, Joe Fichera works in the cockpit of the Focke-Wulf. With the fuselage now treated against corrosion, the restorers turn their attention to wiring, instruments, and countless other components. The wheeled frame constructed to support the fuselage allows rotation about the longitudinal axis and easy movement within the shop. (SI 83-2301-36)

Joe Fichera puts the finishing touches on one of the four ETC 50 wing bomb racks. Here as everywhere, original methods of manufacture are carefully duplicated. If replacement parts are used, they are marked as such and dated. (SI 83-14308-28A)

In the paint shop, Mike carefully transfers the outline of German national insignia from a tracing made before restoration began. Panel lines and other traced references ensure proper positioning of details as the restored aircraft is repainted. (SI 83-6809-34)

The Focke-Wulf nears completion late in the summer of 1983. (SI 83-8079-3A)

Mike Lyons adds yet more authenticity to the restoration by inserting a German medical kit into the appropriate slot. Still being manufactured in Germany, the kit is identical to those used by the Luftwaffe during World War II. (SI 84-14374-30)

seem volatile at all. It gives German aircraft a distinctive smell. If you stick your head into the Ju 388 [in storage awaiting restoration at the Garber Facility] you notice it; it smells a bit like a cup of motor oil."

When time came for the installation of armament, Mike Lyons and Joe Fichera visited the Museum's high-security storage area and chose two 20-mm aircraft cannon that were in worse condition than the others. Their thinking was that these could use restoration immediately, whereas the others could go much longer without attention. During the clean-up, markings were exposed to show how serendipitous their selection had been, for these were the very weapons removed from 931 884 many years before.

There are tours of the Garber Facility every day of the week. During one tour, a German visitor stated that World War II-style medical kits are still being manufactured in Germany. Museum personnel immediately wrote to the manufacturer, and to their great pleasure received a kit that both fit the airplane and satisfied Curator of Flight Materiel Glen Sweeting.

It was put back into the Fw 190 to make it appear as combat-ready as possible. With the acquisition of a rare ETC 501 bomb rack (described below), only a gun camera now remains to be found; Museum curators still maintain high hopes that this rare item may also turn up someday.

Throughout the restoration, internal surfaces were painstakingly treated against long-term corrosion, an eventuality that didn't worry builders who hardly expected the warplane to last two years. Where unprimed dissimilar metals were bolted together (in effect forming a low-voltage battery and promoting electrolytic corrosion), craftsmen chromated the facing surfaces before reattaching them. Where bare metal showed, they applied clear preservatives that would protect but not alter the original appearance.

A question frequently asked is whether aircraft of the National Air and Space Museum are actually put back into flying condition. As is the case with almost all NASM restorations, this rare Focke-Wulf is better than when it rolled out of the factory because of the additional attention given to corrosion control and long-term survival. However, because of preservatives coating all internal surfaces, it would be a very involved process to make the F-8 fly again. One would have to tear down the engine again to cleanse it of preservatives, flush fuel and oil lines (there are no hydraulic lines in the all-electric Fw 190); put in fuel, oil, brake fluid, and a fresh

Focke-Wulf Fw 190 F-8, W.-Nr. 931 884, sits in warm Maryland sunshine on October 11, 1983, after 13,458 man-hours of intensive labor. The fourth roll-out in a career shrouded in mystery, this aircraft lacks only its fuselage bomb rack. The rare ETC 501 was missing from the restoration, and no drawings could be located by which to fabricate a duplicate. (SI 83-145217)

battery; remove the oleo strut supports (used to achieve proper landing gear extension without putting pressure on the seals); reinsert the propeller key (which is removed so that if the propeller is turned, the pistons won't scrape preservatives off the cylinder walls); and go.

People also often ask if there were any surprises; with the Fw 190 project the answer is an emphatic yes. During initial disassembly, the restoration team found that somewhere along the line someone had forgotten to remove the German explosive shell used for emergency canopy jettisoning. A military demolition team trained to deal with old and potentially unstable explosives safely removed and deactivated it.

As is the case with every restoration, the magnitude of the project makes it seem as if it will never be finished. Home stretch on the Focke-Wulf was blessed with beautiful fall weather. Begun in 1980, the restoration project officially ended (except for restoration and installation of a bomb rack) on October 11, 1983, after 13,458 man-hours of dedicated labor. For the *fourth* time in its remarkable career, this sleek German fighter—one of the last of its kind—was rolled out of the factory into the open air.

The restoration team poses in front of the completed Fw 190 F-8: From left to right are Bayne Rector, Joe Fichera, Karl Heinzel, Dale Bucy, Rich Horigan, Reid Ferguson, Mike Lyons, and Kena O'Connor. (SI 86-3822)

Newly restored, Focke-Wulf Fw 190 F-8, W.-Nr. 931 884 again wears the colorful markings and camouflage with which it flew operationally against Soviet forces in World War II. (NASM)

With four 50-kg bombs under the wings and a 250-kg bomb under the fuselage, the National Air and Space Museum's Fw 190 F-8 again appears ready for combat on the eastern front in 1944–45. (NASM)

A different view of the Smithsonian Fw 190 F-8 illustrates the bomb rack and bombs restored by Karl Heinzel and others. (NASM)

Instruments, canopy crank, stick, rudder pedals, and Revi gunsight are among the details visible in this view of the cockpit of the NASM Fw 190 F-8. The illusion of an uneven instrument panel brow is actually wide-angle lens distortion. (NASM)

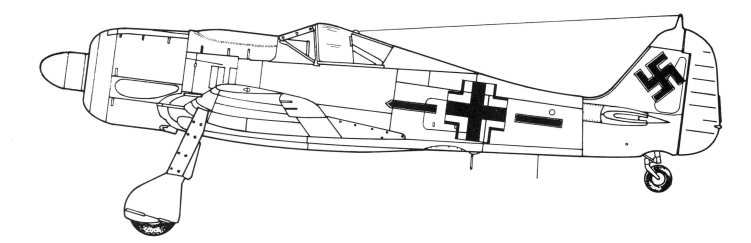

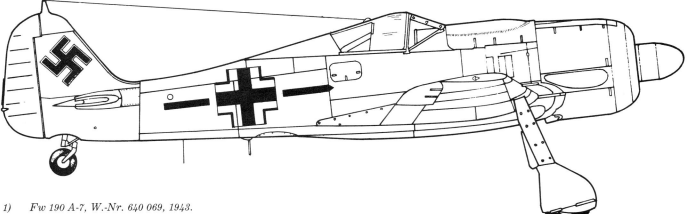

1) Fw 190 A-7, W.-Nr. 640 069, 1943.
   [Left and right side views]

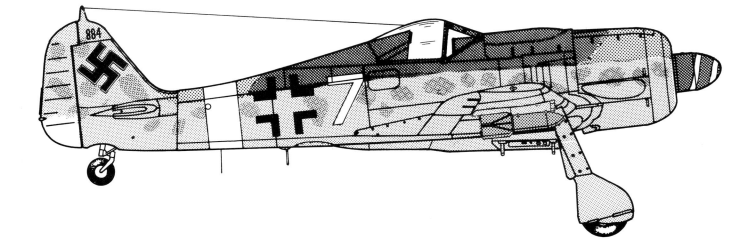

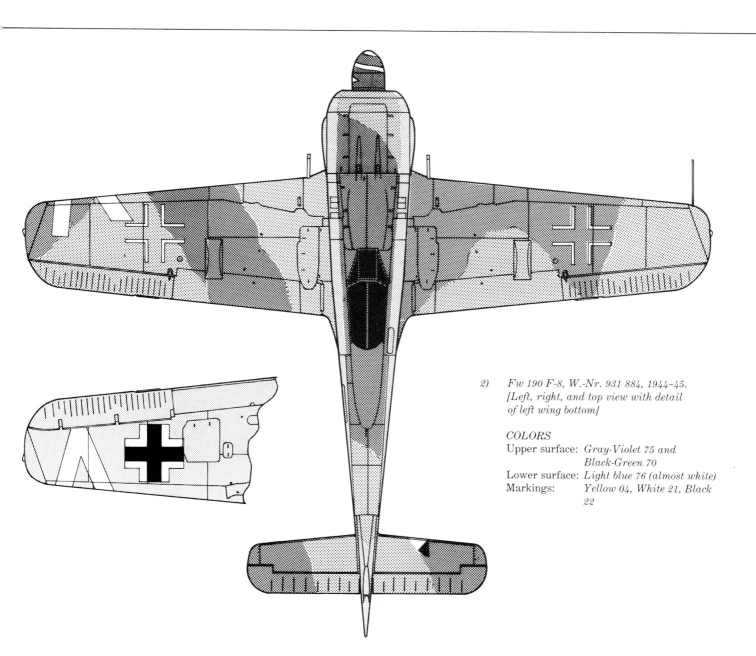

2)   Fw 190 F-8, W.-Nr. 931 884, 1944–45.
     [Left, right, and top view with detail
     of left wing bottom]

COLORS
Upper surface: *Gray-Violet 75 and
                  Black-Green 70*
Lower surface: *Light blue 76 (almost white)*
Markings: *Yellow 04, White 21, Black
                  22*

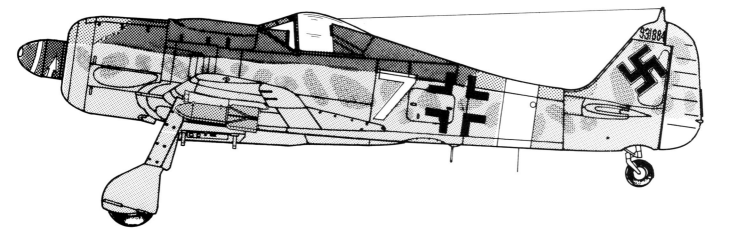

3)   *Fw 190 F-8, W.-Nr. 931 884, spring
      1945.
      [Left and right side views]*

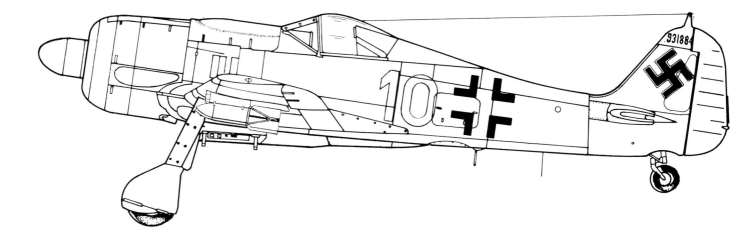

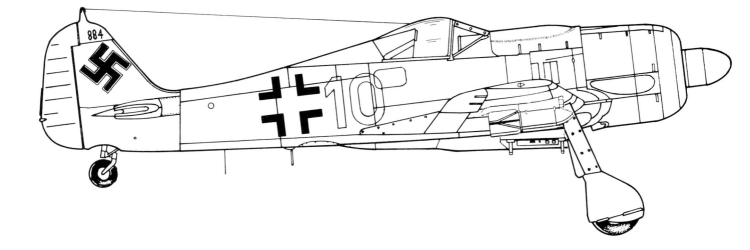

4) *Fw 190 F-8, W.-Nr. 931 884,*
    postwar paint schemes, 1945–46.
    [Left and right side views]

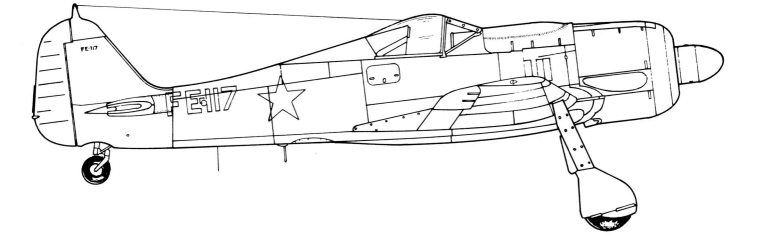

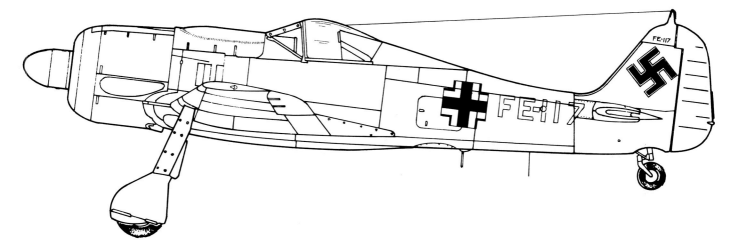

1. *Drawings by Robert C. Mikesh.*
Reproductions may be obtained by
writing to:

Information Management Division
National Air and Space Museum
Smithsonian Institution
Washington, D.C. 20560

The author displays the frame and
housing of an ETC 501 bomb rack
salvaged from a Norwegian
mountainside. Donated by the
Forsvarsmuseet in Oslo and delivered
by the Norwegian air force in 1985,
this critical acquisition allowed the
NASM Fw 190 F-8 to be made at last
truly representative of its wartime
role of ground attack. (SI 85-14202-35)

Postscript
Finishing Touches

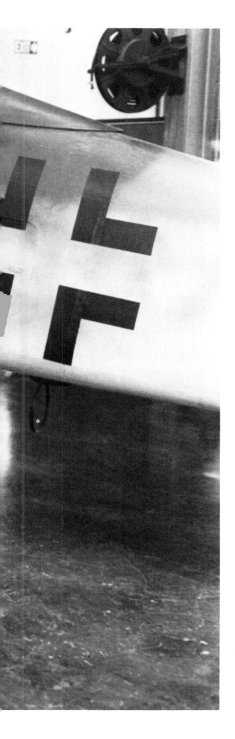

I t was a late-June day in 1985, with airbrushed cumulus clouds in a cerulean sky. At the open front of the Garber Facility's Building 10, the nose of a Focke-Wulf poked into the sunshine. For Karl Stein, it was a poignant reunion that he articulated in fluent English with soft German overtones. After examining every part of the machine and running his hands over the smooth contours, he climbed into the snug cockpit with a lithe spring that bespoke practiced ease.

Slim and still youthful, Stein buried his head for long minutes as he took stock of instruments and controls, remembering check lists, techniques, the feel of the stick and rudder in flight, and countless other details. With them came memories of combat operations on the Russian front.

This visit by a former ground attack pilot was very valuable to Museum personnel, for Stein's memory of the Focke-Wulf and its systems was comprehensive. He confirmed that it was indeed not an original-production F-8, but rather an earlier airframe rebuilt to this configuration. This-should-be-here and that-should-be-there were the thrusts of his statements. The red emergency electrical system cutoff, for example, is to the left whereas on his wartime F-8s it was over on the right side.

Karl Stein also clarified points of operational use of eastern front Focke-Wulfs that had interested Museum personnel. The small blue high-pressure oxygen cylinders in the rear fuselage, visible through the left-side access hatch, were left as installed by the factory, he stated, but were never filled. Supplemental oxygen was not required for the relatively low altitudes at which ground support missions were flown; more significantly, empty tanks could not explode when hit by enemy fire.

At the time of Stein's visit, negotiations were in progress with a group of Norwegians to obtain the ETC 501 bomb rack missing from NASM's otherwise finished Focke-Wulf. It all began with Halvor Sperbund, who had observed in a magazine article that this rare component was missing from the American machine. One of a group undertaking the restoration of another Focke-Wulf Fw 190 F-8, he proposed donating one of several such units to the Museum, a plan supported by the project's mentor, Colonel Finn Lillevik of the Norwegian Air Force.

This Norwegian machine, W.-Nr. 931 862, is truly a sister ship to the NASM F-8, their tail numbers being just twenty-two digits apart. Flown by Unteroffizier Heinz Orlowski of 9./JG 5, *Weisse 1* (white 1) was shot down on February 9, 1945, while attacking a group of RAF Beaufighters (with Mustang escort) attacking a German convoy hiding in a Norwegian fjord. Orlowski, bailing out of his burning plane little more than three hundred feet above ground level, landed in a snowy hillside and miraculously survived even though his parachute had not yet fully opened.

Less fortunate was Leutnant Rudi Linz of the wing's twelfth Staffel (based with the ninth at Herdla, the Luftwaffe airfield near Bergen,

Norway). Damaged by the Beaufighter he shot down, the seventy-victory ace died in the steep crash that followed. It is from the wreck of his Focke-Wulf, *Blaue 4* (blue 4), that Sperbund's group salvaged an ETC 501; team member Arne Navstdalsli carried this unit on his shoulder some ten miles down a Norwegian mountainside.

Halvor Sperbund drove the bomb rack to Oslo, where it boarded a Norwegian air force Lockheed C-130 Hercules transport for delivery to the United States. It arrived on September 3, 1985, at Andrews Air Force Base outside Washington, D.C. The National Air and Space Museum now had an incredibly rare component vital to the completion of its Fw 190F, one impossible to duplicate as no drawings are known to exist. To the selfless Norwegians who worked together to make the gift goes the boundless and heartfelt gratitude of NASM personnel. Future cooperation between Norway and the United States will certainly include NASM assistance in the restoration of their Focke-Wulf.

The steel rack was covered with superficial rust, but was complete and in otherwise excellent condition. Shortly after it was unwrapped, it was lifted into place under the Focke-Wulf where it fit perfectly into the existing mounting lugs. Karl Heinzel and Dale Bucy constructed a new solenoid housing with shackle and sway braces. They worked primarily from photographs as no construction drawings or detailed descriptions of the ETC 501 were available.

As was the case with the Fw 190 A-8, on which later-model F-8 production was based, the bomb rack of FE-117 mounted slightly forward of the location revealed in most photographs of bomb-carrying Focke-Wulfs. This repositioning, obviously performed as a center-of-gravity adjustment, confirmed again the identity of this machine as a later-production entry in the model series.

A new sheet metal fairing was required for the restored rack. The twisted section of the original that Halvor Sperbund had also sent served as the pattern for the new one, and ensured that the proper construction method was used. Screw holes on the underside of the Focke-Wulf provided the exact shape and mounting method, facilitating construction and installation.

The ETC 501 fuselage bomb rack is the only part of the completed machine whose history is known. Its incorporation into the restoration meant that Focke-Wulf Fw 190 F-8/R1 *Weisse 7,* Werk-Nummer 931 884, was at last again truly representative of its participation in World War II. This survivor of the Russian front and other campaigns not known will remain for future generations to wonder at, a tangible piece of history in the rich and diverse collections of the Smithsonian Institution.

Glossary of German Terms

Abwurfbehälter	Cluster bomb
Aufklärung	Reconnaissance
Bereitschaft	Readiness
Blitz	Lightning
Blitzkrieg	Lightning war
Einsatz	Operation; mission
Einsatzbereitschaft	Operational readiness; state of alert
Erprobung	Test
Erprobungsstelle	Test center; the Luftwaffe's primary aircraft test center was at Rechlin (today East Germany)
Feldwebel	Sergeant (see appendix 4)
Flak	*Flieger-Abwehr-Kanone* = Anti-aircraft cannon
Flieger	Flier or pilot; also private (see appendix 4)
Fliegerei	Flying
Fliegerkorps	Air Division
Flug	Flight, n.
Flugkapitän	Title of experienced civilian test pilots
Flugzeug	Aircraft
Flugzeugbau	Aircraft factory
Freiherr	Baron
FuG	Prefix (abbreviation of "Funk-Gerät") denoting radio or electronic equipment
Gefecht	Battle; combat
Gefechtsreihe	Battle row line-astern formation
Gefechtsverband	Battle unit
Generalleutnant	Major general or air vice marshal (see appendix 4)
Generalluftzeugmeister	General in charge of aviation procurement
Generalmajor	Brigadier general or air commodore (see appendix 4)
Geschwader	Wing (organizational unit)
GM 1	Nitrous oxide (laughing gas), used to boost engine power at high altitudes
Gruppe	Group (organizational unit)
Hauptmann	Captain or flight lieutenant (see appendix 4)
Heer	Army
Jabo-Rei	Extended-range fighter bomber (from *Jadgbomber mit vergrösserter Reichweite*)
Jagd-	Fighter (prefix); i.e., *Jagdflugzeug* = fighter plane
Jagdbomber	Fighter-bomber aircraft
Jasta	*Jagdstaffel* = fighter squadron (WWI)
Kampf-	Bomber (prefix); i.e., *Kampfgeschwader* = bomber wing
Kette	Flight of aircraft
Kommandogerät	Control device for BMW 801D engine
Leutnant	Second lieutenant or pilot officer (see appendix 4)
Luftflotte	Air fleet
Luftwaffe	Air force (in German, may refer to the air force of any nationality)

Major	Major or squadron leader (see appendix 4)
Nahkampf	Close support
Oberst	Colonel or group captain (see appendix 4)
Oberstleutnant	Lieutenant colonel or wing commander (see appendix 4)
Pak	*Panzer-Abwehr-Kanone* = antitank cannon
Panzer	Tank (vehicle) or armor
Panzerbekämpfungsstaffel	Antitank squadron
Panzerblitz	Antitank air-to-ground rocket
Reichsverteidigung	Home defense
Reichweite	Range
Revi	Reflecting gun sight (*Reflexvisier*)
Ritterkreuz	Knight's Cross (military decoration)
Rotte	Two-plane element
Schlacht	Ground attack (literally, "slaughter")
Schlachtflieger	Ground attack pilot(s)
Schlachtgeschwader	Ground attack wing (prefix is *SG*)
Schule	School
Schwarm	Four-plane "finger-four" fighter formation
Stab	Staff
Staffel	Squadron
Storch	"Stork" (Fieseler Fi 156 observation aircraft)
Stuka	Dive bomber; in German often, and in English always, used to denote Junkers Ju 87 aircraft (*Sturzkampf*)
Unteroffizier	Staff sergeant or corporal (see appendix 4)
Verteidigung	Defense
Wehrmacht	Military forces
Weihe	Kite (Focke-Wulf Fw 58 liaison aircraft)
Werk-Nummer (W.-Nr.)	Serial number

Fw 190 F-8 Specifications and Performance

Role	Ground attack; close-support fighter-bomber operations	
Wing span	34 ft 5 ½ in	(10.5 m)
Wing area	197 sq ft	(18.3 sq m)
Length	29 ft, 6 in	(9.00 m)
Height	13 ft, 0 in	(3.96 m)
Stabilizer span	11 ft 11 4/3 in	(3,650 mm)
Wheel track	11 ft 5 ¾ in	(3,500 mm)
Engine	BMW 801 D-2, 14-cylinder air-cooled, twin-row radial, 1,730 hp at take-off	
Propeller	VDM 9-12176A three blade, constant speed diameter 10 ft, 11 ¾ in (3,300 mm)	
Fuel supply[1]	140 U.S. gal	(530 l)
Empty weight	6,750 lb	(3060 kg)
Gross weight	10,725 lb[2]	(4865 kg)
Armament (standard)	Fuselage: Two 13-mm MG 131 machine guns Wings: Two 20-mm MG 151 cannon	
Maximum speed	400 mph at 22,000 ft	(644 km/h at 6,700 m)
Service ceiling	34,000 ft	(10,360 m)
Climb to altitude	9.35 min to 20,000 ft	(6,100 m)
Range with maximum fuel	850 mi	(1,370 km)
Range with maximum bomb load	380 mi	(610 km)
Endurance at 6,500 ft (2,000 m) at 280 mph (450 km/h)		2 hr

1. Fw 190 F-8 and F-9 aircraft had a third fuselage tank that increased internal fuel capacity by 25.3 gal (96 l) over earlier Focke-Wulfs. Fw 190 A-8 and A-9 fighters, similarly equipped, had the option of filling the third tank either with fuel or GM 1 (nitrous oxide for injection to boost altitude performance).
2. The F-series had an additional 794 lb (360 kg) of armor to protect its engine, oil tank, and other vulnerable areas from ground fire. To partially offset this weight, as well as that of wing and fuselage bomb racks, two 20-mm wing cannon were installed in the Fw 190F instead of the four standard for the Fw 190A.

Fw 190 F-8 Restoration Man-Hours

Chemical treatment (corrosion control)	1,718
Cockpit	1,109
Cowling	112
Empennage	376
Engine	2,074
Final assembly	1,295
Fuselage	3,176
Planning and ancillary requirements	1,818
Wing/stabilizer/control surfaces	1,926
Total man-hours	13,604

Equivalent Ranks[1]

Luftwaffe	U.S. Army Air Forces	Royal Air Force
Flieger	Private	Aircraftman second class
Gefreiter	Private first class	Aircraftman first class
Obergefreiter	Corporal	Leading aircraftman
Hauptgefreiter	Sergeant	
Unteroffizier	Staff sergeant	Corporal
Unterfeldwebel		
Feldwebel	Technical sergeant	Sergeant
Oberfeldwebel	Master sergeant	Flight sergeant
Stabsfeldwebel	Flight officer	Warrant officer
Leutnant	Second lieutenant	Pilot officer
Oberleutnant	First lieutenant	Flying officer
Hauptmann	Captain	Flight lieutenant
Major	Major	Squadron leader
Oberstleutnant	Lieutenant colonel	Wing commander
Oberst	Colonel	Group captain
Generalmajor	Brigadier general	Air commodore
Generalleutnant	Major general	Air vice marshal
General der Flieger	Lieutenant general	Air marshal
Generaloberst	General (four star)	Air chief marshal
Generalfeldmarschall	General (five star)	Marshal of the Royal Air Force

1. Alfred Price, *Luftwaffe Handbook* (New York: Charles Scribner's Sons, 1977), p. 108.

APPENDIX **5**

Ground Attack Radio Terminology[1]

The terms below are those used by Schlachtflieger for interplane communications during operational ground attack missions on the eastern front during World War II. It was a language of their own, different from that of the fighter and bomber pilots. The function of their code was not to confuse Soviet opposition (anything overheard could not be acted upon in time to be of any use), but rather to facilitate understanding. Multisyllabic and distinct, these code words or phrases generally suggested the German text they replaced.

Code word/phrase	Literal translation	Clear German	Meaning
Ampulle	ampule	Angriff	attack
Ampullle Richardus	ampule Richardus	Angriff wiederholen	repeat attack
Arthur	Arthur (proper name)	Artillerie	artillery
Augustus	Augustus (proper name)	Aufklärer	reconnaissance aircraft
Auto	automobile	Ausweichhafen	aircraft dispersal
Blaue Truppen	blue troops	Eigene Truppen	own troops
Falter	butterfly	Entfaltung	deployment
Feuerzauber	fire magic	Flak	flak
Hallo	hey	Höhe	height
Hallo Toni	hey Tony	Höhe 1 to 100 m	height 0 to 330 ft.
Hallo 23	hey 23	Höhe 2300 m	Height 7,550 ft.
Indianer	Indians	Feindlich	enemy
Ingo	————	Infanterie	infantry
Kondor	condor	Befehl ausgeführt	order carried out
Kurfürst	prince	Kurs	course or heading
Labetrunk	refreshing drink	Landung	landing
Motto	motto	Motorisiert	motorized
Möbelwagen	furniture vans	Kampfflugzeuge	bombers
Napoli	naples	Achtung Nebel	caution fog
Natron	bicarbonate of soda	Nicht verstanden	not understood
Otto	Otto (proper name)	Standort; Bezugspunkt	location; station; map reference point

Code word/phrase	Literal translation	Clear German	Meaning
Piraten	pirates	*Jäger*	fighters
Radfahrer	bicyclists	*Eigen*	own forces
Raupe	caterpillar	*Raum*	area
Richardus	Richardus (proper name)	*Wiederholung*	repeat
Rote Truppen	red troops	*Feindliche Truppen*	enemy troops
Sago	sago palm	*Sammeln*	assemble; regroup
Sagoraupe	sago caterpillar	*Sammelraum*	staging area
Silberstreifen	silver lining	*Sicht*	visibility
Solotanz	solo dance	*Start*	take-off
Stola wachs	stole waxes	*Stellungswechsel*	frequency change
Strato	_____	*Strasse*	street
Triosago	trio sago palm	*Truppenansamm-lung*	troop concentration
Verdol	_____	*Vordere Linie*	front line
Vitamine	vitamin	*Verstanden*	understood
Wartesaal	waiting room	*Warten*	stand by
Wilhelma	Wilhelma (proper name)	*Widerstandsnest*	pocket of resistance
Wolga Hallo	Volga hey	*Wolkenhöhe*	cloud height

1. Bruno Meyer, "Einsatz von Schlachtfliegern" [Operation of ground attack pilots], historical study, March 24, 1953, ref. K113.3019-3, HQ, USAF Historical Research Center, Maxwell AFB, Alabama, pp. 18–19.

Fw 190 Serial Numbers[1]

No official Fw 190 serial number (Werk-Nummer) lists are known to exist, although partial lists have been assembled from photographs and surviving wartime documentation. The Luftwaffe's original serial numbering system gave way around the beginning of 1943—during Fw 190 A-5 production—to a new six-digit system. Following is a reconstruction of production blocks for this latter system:

Fw 190 A-5	Fw 190 A-6	Fw 190 A-7	Fw 190 A-8	Fw 190 A-9
150 000	470 000	340 000	170 000	200 000
150 000	530 000	430 000	171 000	201 000
160 000	531 000	431 000	172 000	202 000
180 000	550 000	432 000	173 000	203 000
410 000	551 000	540 000	174 000	205 000
500 000	670 000*	640 000	175 000	206 000
505 000		642 000	176 000	207 000
710 000		643 000	177 000	209 000
840 000			178 000	380 000***
			179 000	690 000***
			350 000	750 000
			352 000	910 000
			380 000**	980 000
			490 000	
			580 000	
			581 000	
			(650 000?)	
			(670 000?)	
			680 000	
			681 000	
			682 000**	
			683 000	
			688 000	
			690 000**	
			730 000	
			731 000	
			732 000	
			733 000	
			734 000	
			737 000	
			738 000	
			739 000	
			960 000	
			961 000**	

Fw 190 D-9	Fw 190 F-3	Fw 190 F-8	Fw 190 F-9
210 000	670 000	(130 000)	420 000
211 000		582 000	424 000
212 000		583 000	426 000
400 000		584 000	428 000
401 000		585 000	(568 000)
500 000		586 000	580 000
600 000		588 000	
601 000		(930 000)	
		931 000	
		932 000	
		933 000	

Fw 190 G-3	Fw 190 G-8
(110 000)	190 000
160 000	

Research is in progress to correlate serial blocks with Fw 190 production. For now, however, it is generally not possible to say which aircraft were built in Focke-Wulf's factories, by AGO at Oschersleben, by Arado at Warnemünde, or by Fieseler in its Kassel plants. The preceding list, which should not be taken to be comprehensive, includes the 640 000 production block, suggesting that the National Air and Space Museum's Fw 190—whose original Werk-Nummer is 640 069—was built as an Fw 190 A-7.

1. The serial data appearing in this table is drawn from the following two sources:
Volkert Bünz, "Die Werknummernblöcke der Fw 190 A-Baureihen" [The serial number blocks of Fw 190 A-production series], *Luftfahrt International,* August 1981, p. 476.
Jean-Yves Lorant and Jean-Bernard Frappé, *Le Focke Wulf 190,* Collection Docavia series, vol. 15 (Paris: Editions Larivière, 1981), pp. 407–8.
*Very few aircraft in this production block.
**Block also includes some A-9 aircraft.
***Block also includes some A-8 aircraft.
Parentheses indicate probable production blocks.

BMW 801D Engine Analysis

This cutaway display illustrates the compact installation of the Focke-Wulf Fw 190's BMW 801 D-2 twin-row radial engine. (SI 86-4371).

The BMW 801 radial engine is the heart of the Fw 190 design. An excellent power plant in a remarkably compact installation, it ranks among the better engines of World War II, despite failings at altitude stemming from limitations in German supercharger technology.

The Munich-based Bayerische Motoren Werke used experience gained in manufacturing Pratt & Whitney Hornet engines under license in the 1930s to develop its own line of twin-row radials in World War II. Although the BMW 801 shows a Pratt & Whitney heritage, it is an original design that incorporates fuel injection and other German features.

A number of innovative measures allow the BMW 801 to be installed in such a small nacelle: First, adequate cylinder cooling is achieved by pressure baffling augmented by a twelve-blade magnesium-alloy geared fan turning at 1.72 times engine RPM (roughly three times propeller speed). Second, the armor-protected oil tank and honeycomb oil cooler are cleverly fitted into the nose bowl. Third, the engine mount ring, a sealed unit of square cross section, doubles as the hydraulic fluid reservoir. Further streamlining was achieved by substituting air vent louvres (above the forward part of the wing on each side) for drag-inducing cowl flaps.

BMW 801 D-2 Specifications

Type	Air-cooled 14-cylinder twin-row radial
Horsepower	1,730 hp at take-off
Displacement	2,562 cu in (42 l)
Bore	6.15 in (156 mm)
Stroke	6.15 in (156 mm)
Compression ratio	7 to 1
Fuel	C 3, 100 octane
Valve actuation	Valves operated through rocker arms and push rods from cam rings in front and rear of crankcase
Valves	One inlet and one exhaust valve per cylinder
Valve springs	Three per valve
Ignition	Dual, two Bosch ZM 14 magneto generators
Spark plugs	Bosch DW 240 ET 7 or Siemens 35 FU 14 two-electrode 14-mm plugs (two per cylinder)
Weights	
Power unit[1]	2,960 lb (1342 kg)
Propeller	390 lb (177 kg)
Nose bowl[2]	252 lb (114 kg)
Cowling[3]	100 lb (45 kg)
Cooling fan	20.5 lb (9.3 kg)

1. Includes complete engine and mount up to airframe attachment points, cowling, cooling fan, oil cooler and tank (empty), and exhaust manifolds.
2. Includes oil cooler and tank, armor plate, and breather valves; excludes thermostat unit and oil.
3. Excludes nose bowl.

Notes

CHAPTER 1

1. Abbreviation for *Diplom-Ingenieur,* a German degree beyond the American master's degree but short of a doctorate in engineering.

2. A low-drag cowling, developed by Fred E. Weick at the National Advisory Committee for Aeronautics in 1928.

3. Short for *Jagdbomber-Reichweite,* or long-range fighter bomber. See Glossary, appendix 1.

CHAPTER 2

1. Both the U.S. Army Air Forces and the Royal Air Force practiced strategic bombardment in World War II, although their interpretation of the concept varied considerably. RAF night attacks were inherently less accurate and inevitably encompassed area bombing. While American bombers never achieved "pickle-barrel accuracy," they did attack specific industrial targets with remarkable precision.

2. Generalleutnant Adolf Galland and Generalmajor Hubertus Hitschhold, *"Entwicklung der Schlachtflieger"* [Development of ground attack], February 1, 1957, ref. K113.3019-3, HQ, USAF Historical Research Center, Maxwell AFB, Alabama, p. 1. (Hereafter referred to as Galland/Hitschhold.)

3. General Giulio Douhet, 1869–1930, military theorist and author of the influential 1921 work *Il Dominio Dell'Aria* [The command of the air].

4. Fully cantilevered wings are those not requiring drag-inducing external strut or wire bracing. The development of such wings permitted greater speeds and represented a major advance in aircraft structures.

5. *Jasta,* the German term for a World War I fighter squadron, was obsolete and no longer used by World War II (see Glossary, appendix 1).

6. *Stuka,* used in English to refer specifically to the Junkers Ju 87, more properly means simply "dive bomber" (see Glossary, appendix 1).

7. For a clear understanding of the eastern air war beyond the scope of this book, the reader is directed to *Red Phoenix: The Rise of Soviet Air Power 1941–1945,* by Von D. Hardesty (Washington, D.C.: Smithsonian Institution Press, 1982).

8. *Zerstörer* (literally "destroyer") was the Luftwaffe term used to designate multi-seat, multi-engine fighter aircraft.

9. The Messerschmitt Me 210 was succeeded by the Me 410. Although the latter was a much better airplane, the accelerated pace of wartime development had outstripped it by the time it entered service in 1943.

10. Galland/Hitschhold, p. 5. Original quotation: "Wenn Richthofen nicht da war, ging es schief."

11. Great Britain, Air Ministry, *The Rise and Fall of the German Air Force 1939–1945* (New York: St. Martin's Press, 1983), p. 212.

12. The Henschel Hs 129 B-3, entering service late in the war, was fitted with a 75-mm cannon. Although used with some success against Soviet tanks, the Hs 129 B-3 suffered from design, performance, and handling deficiencies that severely limited its production.

13. Luftwaffe pilots adopted the name Soviet pilots had for themselves, calling their enemies "rotte Falken."

14. Oberst Ernst Kupfer, "Schlachtflieger, Panzerjagd und Störflugzeuge im Jahre 1943" [Ground attack, antitank and nuisance aircraft in the year 1943], September 10, 1943, ref. K113.3019-3, HQ, USAF Historical Research Center, Maxwell AFB, Alabama, p. 19. Original quotation: "Bei den Russen schießt ja alles."

15. Ibid., p. 22.

16. Ibid., p. 23.

17. General Karl Koller, *"Umrüstung der Schlachtflieger"* [Conversion of ground attack pilots], excerpt from official diary, June 20, 1944, ref. K113.3019-3, HQ, USAF Historical Research Center, Maxwell AFB, Alabama.

18. Karl Stein, interview with author, June 24, 1985.

19. Galland/Hitschhold, p. 7.

20. One did not have to hold the rank of general to be General der Schlachtflieger, just as one does not have to hold the rank of captain to be the captain of a navy vessel.

21. Great Britain, Air Ministry, "Some Notes on G.A.F. Ground Attack (Schlacht) Units," A.D.I.(K) Report No. 242A/1945, ref. 512.619B-28, HQ, USAF Historical Research Center, Maxwell AFB, Alabama, p. 1.

22. Quoted passages are from Kupfer, "Schlachtflieger, Panzerjadg und Störflugzeuge."

23. An interesting view of Rudel is presented by former SG 2 pilot Fritz Seyffardt (see chapter 3). In a letter to the author dated November 19, 1985, Seyffardt recalls his former commander as having been an *Einzelkämpfer* (individual fighter) unsuited to command of a large unit. His postwar activities and unrepentant views were seen as "false" by Seyffardt, who adds that he and other former pilots regarded their late Kommandeur "as politically naive and childish."

24. Hans Ulrich Rudel, *Stuka Pilot* (Dublin: Euphorion Books, 1952), p. 172.

25. Hubertus Hitschhold, "Die Schlachtfliegerei in der deutschen Luftwaffe" [Ground attack in the German air force], historical study, February 12, 1957, ref. K113.3019-3, HQ, USAF Historical Research Center, Maxwell AFB, Alabama, p. 5.

26. The *Ritterkreuz* or Knight's Cross was the highest German military decoration; greater recognition still came with the award of the supplementary *Eichenlauben* (Oak Leaves) and *Schwertern* (Swords).

27. Kupfer, "Schlachtflieger, Panzerjagd und Störflugzeuge," p. 9.

28. Bruno Meyer, *"Einsatz von Schlachtfliegern"* [Operation of ground attack pilots], historical study, March 24, 1953, ref. K113.3019-3, HQ, USAF Historical Research Center, Maxwell AFB, Alabama, pp. 18–19.

29. Hitschhold, "Die Schlachtfliegerei," p. 13.

Chapter 3

1. Heinz Lange to author, August 7, 1985.

2. Fritz Seyffardt to author, October 9, 1985.

3. The Immelmann Geschwader, more significant and illustrious than the earlier Schlachtgeschwader 2, was activated in October 1943. The earlier SG 2, disbanded the previous month, had fought on the eastern front with Fw 190s and Henschel Hs 129s.

4. Peter Traubel to author, June 21, 1985.

5. Stein, June 24, 1985.

6. Karl Stein, interview with Dr. Von D. Hardesty, January 10, 1980.

7. Ibid.

8. Ibid.

9. Ibid.

10. Ibid.

11. Stein, June 24, 1985.

12. John Jarmy, telephone interview with author, November 6, 1985.

13. Rudel, *Stuka Pilot*, p. 156.

14. Adolf Galland to author, May 6, 1985.

15. Barry Mahon, telephone interview with author, June 7, 1985.

16. Ibid.

17. Short for *Kriegsgefangener* (prisoner of war), the term *Kriegie* was used by captured Allied airmen to describe themselves.

18. Eric Brown, *Wings of the Luftwaffe: Flying German Aircraft of the Second World War* (London: Jane's Publishing, 1977), p. 78.

19. Ibid., p. 81.

20. Ibid., p. 84.

21. "A General Comparative Performance of the German FW-190 and the American P-51," U.S. Army Air Forces [July 1942], NASM microfilm document collection, Reel 8097, Frame 97 (IP 97), Washington, D.C.

22. Jack Ilfrey and Max Reynolds, *Happy Jack's Go-Buggy: A WWII Fighter Pilot's Personal Document,* foreword by Eddie Rickenbacker (Hicksville, N.Y.: Exposition Press, 1979), p. 91.

23. Jack Ilfrey to author, May 28, 1985.

24. Jack Ilfrey, telephone interview with author, July 5, 1985.

25. Richard J. Lee to author, September 9, 1985.

26. Ibid.

27. Robert S. Johnson and Martin Caidin, *Thunderbolt!* (New York: Rinehart & Company, 1958), p. 121.

28. Ibid., p. 181.

29. Ibid., pp. 184–85.

30. William R. O'Brien, "Encounter Report," USAAF intelligence debriefing, March 5, 1944, ref. SQ-FI-363-HI, HQ, USAF Historical Research Center, Maxwell AFB, Alabama.

31. William R. O'Brien to author, July 15, 1985.

32. Charles E. Yeager and Leo Janos, *Yeager: An Autobiography* (New York: Bantam Books, 1985), p. 83.

33. Gustav E. Lundquist to author, January 2, 1986.

34. Ibid.

35. Kenneth Chilstrom to author, June 5, 1985.

36. "Captured Aircraft Equipment Report No. 14: Report of Comparative Combat Evaluation of Focke-Wulf 190-A-4 [*sic*] Airplane," U.S., Department of the Navy, Record Group 255 (NACA), ref. 1105.4, National Archives, Suitland, Maryland, April 1944.

37. Arthur G. Johnson to author, June 21, 1985.

38. Ibid.

39. John J. Voll, telephone interview with author, June 10, 1985.

40. "Max" Lamb's citation for award of the Silver Star (Oak-Leaf Cluster) by the Ninth Air Force (June 15, 1945) reads:

> George M. Lamb, O-730537, Major, Air Corps, 354th Fighter Group. For gallantry in action on 23 March 1945. While flying in

conjunction with the newly established crossing of the Rhine River Maj LAMB distinguished himself by superior aerial proficiency and brilliant leadership. When a superior force of enemy aircraft threatened the safety of a pontoon bridge Maj LAMB vigorously led a squadron of eight P-51 type aircraft to attack the enemy; and despite overwhelming odds he personally destroyed three hostile planes while under his brilliant leadership a total of nine enemy aircraft were destroyed and the enemy completely routed. The superior pilotage, aggressiveness and determination exhibited by Maj LAMB on this occasion are exemplary of the highest traditions of the Army Air Forces.

41. George M. Lamb to author, May 24, 1985.

CHAPTER 4

1. Oliver P. Echols, Memorandum to director of AAF Air Technical Service Command, April 4, 1945, "Captured Enemy Equipment: Freeman Field 1945–46," Archival Support Center, NASM, Washington, D.C.

2. Paul H. Kemmer, Memorandum to TSCON, April 28, 1945, "Captured Enemy Equipment 1942-43-44-45," Archival Support Center, NASM, Washington, D.C.

3. Echols, "Captured Enemy Equipment."

4. The prefixes EB and FE stand for Evaluation Branch and Foreign Equipment, respectively.

5. FE-118, an Fw 190 D-13, also survives and is today on display at the Champlin Fighter Museum in Mesa, Arizona.

CHAPTER 5

1. Michael Lyons, interview with author, October 14, 1983.

2. Dale Bucy, interview with author, October 14, 1983.

3. Lyons.

4. Bucy.

5. Joseph Fichera, interview with author, October 14, 1983.

6. See Robert C. Mikesh and Osamu Tagaya, *Moonlight Interceptor: Japan's "Irving" Night Fighter*, Famous Aircraft of the National Air and Space Museum Series, vol. 8 (Washington, D.C.: Smithsonian Institution Press, 1985).

Bibliography

The greatest contribution any new volume on the Focke-Wulf Fw 190 may make is to bring new information before the public. With this intent in mind, it may be stated that the heart of this work is chapter 2—Schlachtfliegerei. To ensure accuracy and detail while addressing the lack of published information on eastern front ground attack operations during World War II, the author has relied almost exclusively on primary source material. Particularly important in chapter 2 were historical analyses by Messrs. Galland, Hitschhold, Kupfer, Maass, and Meyer, held in the keeping of the United States Air Force at Maxwell Air Force Base, Montgomery, Alabama. Formerly classified British intelligence summaries located at this research center and at the National Archives also yielded valuable clues.

Additional primary information came to light within the collection of the National Air and Space Museum itself: bound volumes of correspondence, memoranda, orders, and letters revealed much heretofore forgotten about the refurbishing and testing of captured aircraft at Wright and Freeman Fields in Ohio and Indiana, respectively.

Finally, great effort was expended in the task of locating and interviewing Allied and Axis ground attack and fighter pilots. Their help, perforce absent from the bibliographic citations but acknowledged in footnotes, was invaluable in confirming points, adding detail, and achieving a balanced historical overview.

The following list represents only those volumes and articles particularly worthwhile or useful to the author in this project. Omitted, but the author hopes not slighted, is a large body of literature on what is certainly one of the most popular fighter aircraft ever produced.

Aders, Gebhard. "Die Focke-Wulf Fw 190: Eine Typenübersicht der Baureihen A, F, G und S" [The Fw 190: A type overview of the production series A, F, G and S]. *Luftfahrt International,* part I, August 1981, pp. 297–304; part II, September 1981, pp. 343–50.

"An Advanced Enemy Fighter." *Aeronautics,* vol. 8, no. 5 (June 1943), pp. 38–41.

Brown, Eric. *Wings of the Luftwaffe: Flying German Aircraft of the Second World War.* London: Jane's Publishing, 1977.

Chant, Christopher. *Ground Attack.* London: Almark Publishing, 1976.

Deichman, Paul. *German Air Force Operations in Support of the Army.* USAF Historical Study No. 163, USAF Historical Division, Research Studies Institute. Maxwell AFB, Alabama: Air University, 1962.

"Design Analysis of Focke–Wulf 190." *Weight Engineering,* vol. 1, no. 3 (winter 1943), pp. 10–13, 25.

Dierich, Wolfgang. *Die Verbände der Luftwaffe 1939–1945* [Units of the Luftwaffe 1939–1945]. Stuttgart: Motorbuch Verlag, 1976.

Fw 190 A-8 Aircraft Handbook. Ottawa: Valkyrie Publications, 1974.

Galland, Adolf, and Hubertus Hitschhold. *"Entwicklung der Schlachtflieger"* [Development of ground attack]. Historical analysis. Ref. K113.3019–3. HQ, USAF Historical Research Center, Maxwell AFB, Alabama, February 1, 1957.

Great Britain, Air Ministry. *The Rise and Fall of the German Air Force 1933–1945.* Introduction by H. A. Probert. Great Britain: His Majesty's Stationery Office, 1948; reprint ed., New York: St. Martin's Press, 1983.

_____. "Crashed Enemy Aircraft: Report Serial No. 191." A.I.2(g) Report, April 19, 1943. U.S. Air Force Museum, Dayton Ohio. (Representative of extensive and informative wartime A.I.2(g) intelligence series.)

_____. "Some Notes on G.A.F. Ground Attack (Schlacht) Units." A.D.I.(K) Report No. 242A/1945. HQ, USAF Historical Research Center, Maxwell AFB, Alabama, ref. 512.619B–28. (Representative of extensive and informative wartime A.D.I.(K) intelligence series.)

Hardesty, Von D. *Red Phoenix: The Rise of Soviet Air Power 1941–1945.* Washington, D.C.: Smithsonian Institution Press, 1982.

Hardesty, Von D., and John T. Greenwood. "Soviet Air Forces in World War II" in *The Soviet Air Forces,* ed. Paul J. Murphy. London: McFarland & Company, 1984.

Hitschhold, Hubertus. *"Die Schlachtfliegerei in der deutschen Luftwaffe"* [Ground attack in the German air force]. Historical study. Ref. K113.3019–3. HQ, USAF Historical Research Center, Maxwell AFB, Alabama, February 12, 1957.

Kupfer, Ernst. "Schlachtflieger, Panzerjagd und Störflugzeuge im Jahre 1943" [Ground attack, antitank and nuisance aircraft in the year 1943]. Transcript of speech. Ref. K113.3019–3. HQ, USAF Historical Research Center, Maxwell AFB, Alabama, September 10, 1943.

Lorant, Jean-Yves, and Jean-Bernard Frappé. *Le Focke Wulf 190.* Collection Docavia series, vol. 15. Paris: Editions Larivière, 1981.

Maass, General. "Die dem Heer im Kriege taktisch unterstellten Verbände der Luftwaffe" [Luftwaffe units tactically subordinate to the army in the war]. Ref. K113.836. HQ, USAF Historical Research Center, Maxwell AFB, Alabama, September 13, 1956.

Meyer, Bruno. "Einsatz von Schlachtfliegern" [Operation of ground attack pilots]. Ref. K113.3019–3. HQ, USAF Historical Research Center, Maxwell AFB, Alabama, March 24, 1953.

Murray, Williamson. *Luftwaffe.* Baltimore: Nautical & Aviation Publishing, 1985.

Nowarra, Heinz. *The Focke-Wulf 190: A Famous German Fighter.* Letchworth, Herts., England: Harleyford Publications, 1965.

_____. *Gezielter Sturz: Die Geschichte der Sturzkampfbomber aus aller Welt* [Aimed dive: The history of dive bombers around the world]. Stuttgart: Motorbuch Verlag, 1982.

Obermaier, Ernst. *Die Ritterkreuzträger der Luftwaffe* [The Knight's Cross holders of the Luftwaffe]. Vol. II: *Stuka und Schlachtflieger* [Stuka and ground attack pilots]. Mainz, West Germany: Verlag Dieter Hoffmann, 1976.

Price, Alfred. *The Fw 190 at War.* New York: Charles Scribner's Sons, 1977.

_____. *Luftwaffe Handbook 1939–1945.* New York: Charles Scribner's Sons, 1977.

Ratley, Lonnie O., III. "A Lesson of History: The Luftwaffe and Barbarossa." *Air University Review,* vol. 34, no. 3 (March-April 1983), pp. 50–65.

Ries, Karl. *Markierungen und Tarnanstriche der deutschen Luftwaffe im 2. Weltkrieg* [Markings and camouflage of the Luftwaffe in World War II]. 4 vols. Mainz: Verlag Dieter Hoffmann, 1963–72.

Rudel, Hans Ulrich. *Stuka Pilot.* Dublin: Euphorion Books, 1952.

Shennan, Anthony, and Geoffrey Pentland. *Focke-Wulf Fw 190 Described.* Series 1, no. 9. Toronto: Kookaburra Technical Publications, 1966.

_____. *Focke-Wulf Fw 190 & Ta 152.* Series 1, no. 9. Dandenong, Victoria, Australia: Kookaburra Technical Publications, 1970.

Shores, Christopher F. *Ground Attack Aircraft of World War II.* London: Macdonald and Jane's, 1977.

Smith, J. Richard, and Antony L. Kay. *German Aircraft of the Second World War*. London: Putnam, 1972.

Tessin, Georg. *Verbände und Truppen der deutschen Wehrmacht und Waffen-SS im Zweiten Weltkrieg 1939–1945* [Units and troops of the German Wehrmacht and Waffen-SS in World War II 1939–1945]. Vol. 14. Osnabrück, West Germany: Biblio Verlag, 1980. Note: while this series consists of more than twenty volumes, only volume 14 covers Luftwaffe units.

Toliver, Raymond F., and Trevor J. Constable. *Fighter Aces of the Luftwaffe*. Fallbrook, Calif.: Aero Publishers, 1977.

U.S., Department of the Army, Air Forces. "A General Comparative Performance of the German FW-190 and The American P-51. . . ." Washington, D.C.: Microfilm Document Collection, National Air and Space Museum, Reel 8097, Frame 97 (IP 97) [July 1942].

_____. *Concept of Russian Air Warfare*. Air Intelligence Report No. 100-66/1-34. Air Force Museum, Wright-Patterson AFB, Ohio, ref. C21/34. Washington, D.C.: Office of the Assistant Chief of Air Staff, April 26, 1946.

_____. "Captured Enemy Aircraft 1936-39-40-41-42-43-44-45." Wright and Freeman Field documentation. Archival Support Center, National Air and Space Museum, Washington, D.C.

_____. "Captured Enemy Equipment 1942-43-44-45." Archival Support Center, NASM, Washington, D.C.

_____. "Captured Enemy Equipment: Freeman Field 1945–46." Wright and Freeman Field documentation. Two unnumbered volumes. Archival Support Center, NASM, Washington, D.C.

U.S., Department of the Navy. "Captured Aircraft Equipment Report No. 14: Report of Comparative Combat Evaluation of Focke-Wulf 190-A-4 [*sic*] Airplane." Record Group 255, ref. 1105.4. National Archives, Suitland, Maryland, April 1944.

Wagner, Wolfgang. *Kurt Tank: Konstrukteur und Testpilot bei Focke-Wulf* [Kurt Tank: Manufacturer and test pilot at Focke-Wulf]. *Die deutsche Luftfahrt* Series vol. 1. Munich: Bernard & Graefe, 1980.

Weber, Eberhard, and Uwe Feist. *Focke-Wulf 190*. Aero Series vol. 18. Fallbrook, Calif.: Aero Publishers, 1968.

Windrow, Martin C. "Focke-Wulf Fw 190A" in *Aircraft in Profile* series, ed. by Martin C. Windrow, vol. 1. Garden City, N.Y.: Doubleday, 1969.

ABOUT THE AUTHOR

Jay P. Spenser is the author of four books and many articles on aviation history. A New Englander who graduated from Middlebury College in Vermont, he learned to fly in his teens. His love of flight brought him to the National Air and Space Museum's Aeronautics Department in 1976, where he served as assistant curator from 1983 to 1986. He now pursues a career as a free-lance writer.